Elder Abuse and Neglect

Elder Abuse and Neglect

Arvind K. Joshi

GYAN

Published, 2021

Published by

Gyan Publishing House
5, Ansari Road
Daryaganj, New Delhi-110002
Phone: 011-47034999, 9811692060
www.gyanbooks.com
E-mail: books@gyanbooks.com

Printed at: Gyan Press, Delhi.

Cataloging in Publication Data—DK
Courtesy: D.K. Agencies (P) Ltd. <docinfo@dkagencies.com>

Joshi, Arvind K. (Arvind Kumar), author.
Elder abuse and neglect / Arvind K. Joshi.
pages cm
Includes bibliographical references.
ISBN 9788121220163

1. Older people—Abuse of—India. 2. Older people—India—Social conditions. 3. Older people—India—Economic conditions. 4. Older people—Health and hygiene—India. I. Title.

LCC HV6626.54.I4J67 2020 | DDC 362.6820954 23

The book is dedicated to my parents late Shri Aditya Swarup Joshi and Late Smt. Krishna Rani Joshi. No words can express my feeling for them and the sacrifices they have made, but this token gesture is the least I can do.

Contents

Preface and Acknowledgements

No doubt, caring for the elderly is one of the *sine qua non* of our ancient Indian civilization and it is still part of our culture. But due to several socio-economic reasons the traditional care and support system is on the decline. Several elderly persons are experiencing abuse and neglect.

Mistreatment with elderly family member and neglecting their care is considered as an act of elder abuse. If family members fail to fulfil their kinship obligations to provide sufficient food, comfortable housing, required health and medical needs and proper care, this also constitute neglect. Elder abuse and neglect is a hidden crime in the family and is emerging as a significant problem, which was unrecognized and certainly unreported. It is unreported because quite often, the perpetrator of this abuse, being their own children, no parents will willingly state that their child is mistreating them. For elderly people, the consequences of abuse can be especially serious. It was found in the recent researches in USA that elders who have been abused tend to die earlier than those who are not abused, even in the absence of chronic conditions of life threatening disease.

The present study aimed at exploring and analysing the nature and extent of elder abuse. The findings will be useful to scholars of different disciplines, policy makers and NGO professionals who deal with aging issues and/or expecially issues relating to elder abuse and neglect.

This book is an outcome of UGC major project. It took almost four years to complete the project work and almost one year to re-check and verify the facts to convert into book form. In the five years that went behind the research taking its final shape, lie the constant encouragement, support and good wishes of several persons. This acknowledgement is a small token of their appreciation and gratitude that I have bear in my heart towards them.

First and formost I would like to acknowledge with thanks the funding support provided by UGC, New Delhi to me on a major project on "Elder Abuse and Neglect: The Hidden Crime in the Family" without which the research would not have been possible.

I wish to express my heartfelt gratitude to Late Prof. B.N. Juyal for his continued guidance, help, support and encouragement at every stage of work. I am obliged to my father late Shri A.S. Joshi for having enthused me to publish a book on my major project work thereby making it available to a larger readership. I am thankful to the Banaras Hindu University for providing me sabbatical leave to do the same.

Very special thanks to my wife Dr. Vibha Joshi, Son Mr. Abhinav Joshi and daughter Ms. Apoorva Joshi for their intellectual support and constant encouragement, without their active support this book would have remained an unfullfilled wish.

Last but not the least, I am thankful to all the senior citizen respondents who have given almost all the information on the sensitive topic and who were always ready to share their experiences and their problems with me in long talks and interviews, without whom the research would not have been possible.

Arvind K. Joshi

List of Tables

List of Figures

Chapter - 1

Introduction

Contemporary society is beset with numerous problems among which the demographic changes occuring all over the world have assumed enormous significance. Apart from the growth of population in almost every society of the developing world, the change in the population structure of the senior citizens is by far the most significant. Not only the longevity in the senior citizens has increased because of the significant development in the medical sciences, changes in the life style of the people and also because of the substantial improvement in health care and welfare mechanism for the senior citizens. At the same time there have been many complicated problems in the protection, welfare and care of the senior citizens, which are becoming the focus of attention and activism among the demographers, economic and social policy planners, and designers of service delivery mechanisms, as also among the large number of voluntary agencies and non- governmental organizations who have interest in the welfare of the aged population in one way or the other. It is an evident fact that the social value structure of the contemporary society is eroding because of the modern forces of change. Urbanization, industrialization, modernization and transformation of the educational scenario of the modern society have affected the basic fabric of the society. The society is moving towards greater individualism and self centered activism. The traditional loyalty to family and kinship organizations and neighborhood are also becoming increasingly weak.

The resultant effect of these far reaching changes has affected the status of senior citizens as individuals and as members of primary group. The traditional way of respect and regard given to the old aged person are being replaced by indifferent and even willfull disregard and thus fostering sense of dependency, neglect and powerlessness among them. The physical infirmity of the senior citizens coupled with loss of earning power has had serious effects on the old aged persons. Thus the senior citizens falling in this category have become isolated and pathetic figures for whom no one has enough time and resource to take proper care.

Due to gradual weakening of primary relationship, reciprocity and trust among the family members, the neglected senior citizens are moving to the old age homes either run by charitable voluntary agencies or sponsored by the state through non-governmental organizations. But these are very inadequate. It was considered that the old age person will have shelter homes where they will get sufficient care, food, medicine etc. In Indian situation such institutional arrangement has become counter-productive. The very concept of old age home is anchored on the premise that the old aged persons are unprotected, insecure and lack food and medicine. However, the working of these organization has indicated that they also need human warmth and psychological gratification which are generally lacking in these bureaucratically run institutions. What an senior citizens could get from his family, near relatives, friends and close acquaintances is missing in the institutional environment of the old aged home.

Thus, the contemporary society has thrown up new problems and new challenges to the ageing population. How to sortout these problems and provide dignified status to the old age persons is a stupendous task before the modern society. As the size of old age population is to increase further in future and the traditional structural capability for the care and welfare of the senior citizens is likely to decrease further, the plight of the senior citizens also in all probability become worse. Therefore, there is an urgent need to understand the changing conditions of senior citizens for which an interdisciplinary paradigm is urgently needed.

Population Ageing

The most important demographic change occurring in the contemporary society is characterized as population ageing. It is correctly said that, "each of us alive now is living in an era of unprecedented global ageing -a worldwide process of change which is happening rapidly and inexrably." (The Ageing and Development Report, 1999: 179) With the rapid changes in the health values, health care delivery system and the changes in the material conditions of life available to individuals, the population of the elders is increasing worldwide. Earlier fertility and death were considered to be natural phenomenon which used to maintain a balance between the younger population and older population. It was considered that the death of the individuals was compensated by the birth of younger ones. The scenario has changed now with the longevity of elders and decline in the fertility of the new generation. The result is that the numbers of elders is increasing in almost every part of the world and with reduced birth rate the younger ones are becoming fewer and fewer in some parts of the world population. This has consequences for the sustenance of elder population which can be offset through longer economic resources and better health care delivery system. The social security for the older population and the support system for the elder either within the family or outside the family in institutionalized settings are under strain. Therefore, the attention of the social scientists, planning administrators and the demographers are now being increasingly focused on the ageing population.

World Population Ageing report (WPA, 2007) emphasize that the population ageing- the process by which older individuals become a proportionally larger share of the total population-was one of the most distinctive demographic event of the 21st century.

The shift in age structure associated in population ageing has a profound impact on economic, political and social conditions. For example concerns are growing about the long term viability of inter-generational social support system which is crucial for the well being of both the older and younger generation. (Cliquet and Nizamudding, 1999). This is especially true where the provision of care within the family becomes more and more difficult as family size decreases as women, who are traditionally main care-givers increasingly engage in employment outside the home.

As more people live longer, retirement, pension and other social benefits tend to extend over longer period of time. This makes it necessary for social security systems to change substantially in order to remain effective. Increasing longevity can also result in rising medical costs and increasing demands for health services, since older people are typically more vulnerable to chronic diseases. (De Jong-Gierveld and Van Solinge, 1995).

The Emerging Scenario of Population Ageing In India

India is undergoing the process of drastic demographic transition. As a result, there is a rising problem of population ageing i.e. a relative increase in the number of aged persons (60+). Demographic transition is, in general, a process of change where society passes through the stages of high fertility and high mortality to low fertility and low mortality. Presently India is at Stage III of the 4 stages of modern transition theory. The welcome trend in demographic transition with an improvement in mortality conditions and substantial reduction on the reproduction front has created an imbalance in the age structure of the population such that the elderly have a bigger share in it (Rajan S. et al. 1999).

Population ageing is affecting every single individual, family, and community. It has considerable implications for the social security system. In near future ageing will emerge as a priority area. Therefore, planning for graceful ageing is required with the assistance of family, community and state. Problems and needs of the elderly can be fulfilled by the well developed social security measures, better medical and health facilities and other suitable care and welfare measures.

Several studies on India have assessed the demographic dynamics of the aged (e.g. Chanana and Talwar, 1987, Bose and Gangrade 1988, Sarkar, 1989, Guha Roy, 1989, Goyal, 1989, Rajan, 1989, 1992, Mari Bhat, 1992, Gulati and Rajan, 1998, 1991, Sharma and Xenos, 1992, Chakraborti, 2004, etc.). The population of the aged, that is, those of the age of 60 years and above is on the increase. In 1971, they were 28 million; in 1981, 42 million; in 1991, 56 million and in 2001, 75 million. It is expected that in 2025 their population will be more than 175 millions. Accordingly, their proportion in the population has gone up. It has risen from 5.63 percent in 1961 to 6.58 in 1991; 7.08 in 2001 and 9.87 in 2021, respectively. The life expectancy at age 60 during 1995-2000 was 16 and 17 years respectively for male and female. The absolute population of the elderly and their proportion is being presented in the following table.

Table 1.1: Population (absolute number) and Proportion (%) of Elderly in India (with projection)

Year	*Absolute Number 60 +*	*Proportion (%) (60+)*	*Proportion (%) 70+*	*Absolute Number (70+)*
1961	2,46,99,125	5.63	1.96	86,05,408
1971	3,26,80,995	5.93	2.08	1,13,29,929
1981	4,15,37,602	6.28	2.31	1,52,99,938
1991	5,56,05593	6.58	2.40	2,025,2219
2001	7,16,97,634	7.08	2.71	2,74,45,338
2011	9,78,69,607	8.18	3.05	3,66,29,667
2021	13,64,58,825	9.87	3.75	5,20,18,105

Source: Rajan et.al. (p. 46-52).

It is obvious from the above table that ageing among elderly is also continuously progressing as in 1961 there were 1.96 percent of 70+ aged persons which grew to 2.71 percent in 2001 and projected to grow further to 3.75 in 2021. Further, the number of centenarians in 1995 was 3000, wherein there were 1000 males and 2000 females. It is expected that their population in 2050 will be 1, 11,000 where in there will be 34,000 males and 77,000 females. (Chakraborti R.D. 2004) In our gender-biased society this feminization of aged population may create another type of problem. Yet, it can be surmised that the scenario might change, as the status of women in India is changing and the process would be accelerated in the coming decades.

Trend in the proportion (%) aged (60 and above years) for males and females in India is presented in the following table.

The Indian population census reported 99,000 centenarians in 1961 their number rose to 138,000 in 1991. The growth rate among different cohorts of elderly such as 60 plus, 70 plus and 80 plus during the decade 1991-2001 was much higher than the general population growth rate of 2 percent per annum during the same period. However, the sex ratio among the elderly in India has favoured males as against the trend prevalent in other parts of the world (Table 1.3 and 1.4).

Table 1.2: Trends in the Proportion (%) Aged (60+) for Males and Females in India (with Projections)

Year	*Male*	*Female*
1961	5.47	5.81
1971	5.94	5.99
1981	6.21	6.36
1991	6.55	6.61
2001	6.97	7.19
2011	8.07	8.29
2021	9.63	10.12

Source: Rajan et.al. (p. 57-58)

Table- 1.3: Number and Proportion of Elderly in the Indian Population by Age Groups, 1961-2001

	Number (in Million)					*Percent of Elderly to the Total Population*				
	1961	*1971*	*1981*	*1991*	*2001*	*1961*	*1971*	*1981*	*1991*	*2001*
60+	25	33	43	57	77	5.6	6.0	6.49	6.76	7.5
70+	9	11	15	21	29	2.0	2.1	2.33	2.51	2.9
80+	2	3	4	6	8	0.6	0.6	0.62	0.76	0.8
90+	0.5	0.7	0.7	1	n.a.	0.1	0.1	0.1	0.2	n.a
100+	0.01	0.01	0.01	0.01	n.a.	0.02	0.02	0.02	0.02	n.a.

Source: S Irudaya Rajan. (2006), "Population Ageing and Health in India"

Percentage share of elderly persons in the population of India is ever increasing since 1961. As per above table it is clear that in 1961, 5.6 percent population was in the age category of 60 years or more, the proportion has increased to 8.6 percent in 2011.

Table-1.4: Sex Ratio and Growth Rate Among the Indian Elderly, 1971-2001

	Sex Ratio of Elderly (males per 1000 females)				*Growth of Elderly (percent)*		
	1971	*1981*	*1991*	*2001*	*1971-81*	*1981-91*	*1991-2001*
60+	1066	1042	1075	1028	2.78	2.72	3.04
70+	1030	1026	1084	991	3.13	3.08	3.32
80+	950	990	1090	1051	2.54	4.35	2.35
90+	897	892	1019	n.a.	0.66	5.08	n.a.
100+	798	844	896	n.a.	0.19	0.44	n.a.

Source: Estimated by S Irudaya Rajan 2006 from last four censuses in "Population Ageing and Health in India"

The sex ratio among elderly people reached up to 1033 in 2011.

The projected population aged 60+ by sex as per the report of the Technical Group on Population Projections constituted by the National Commission on Population, May 2006 published by the Office of the Registrar General, India (Source: NISD, January 2008: 1) is as under:

Table 1.5: The Projected Population 60+, India (in millions)

Year	*Males*	*Females*	*Persons*
2006	40.75	42.83	83.58
2011	48.14	50.33	98.47
2016	58.11	59.99	118.10
2021	70.60	72.65	143.25
2026	84.62	88.56	173.18

India is one of the few countries in the world where males outnumber females. This phenomenon among the elderly is intriguing because female life expectancy at ages 60 and 70 is slightly higher than that of males. Available findings on ageing suggest that fertility has played a predominant role in the ageing process compared to mortality. In India, there has been a substantial reduction compared to fertility. In 1950, there were 5.2% male who were 60 +, 2.9 percent were 65+ and 1.7 percent were 70+. In 2000 for each of these cohorts the proportion increases i.e. 8.0 percent in 60 + category, 3.5 percent in 65+ category and 3.0 percent among male belongings to 70+ category. Among the female there has been much higher growth. In 1950 there were 6.1 percent in female category, in 65+ category across 3.8 and in 70+ category it was 2 percent. The corresponding proportion in 2000 it was 8.9 percent in 60+ category, 5.9 percent in 65+ category and 3.4 percent in 70+ category for female.

The percentage share of the projected population aged 60+ in the total projected population by Sex is as under:

Table 1.6: The Percentage share of Projected Population 60+, India

Year	*Males*	*Females*	*Persons*
2006	7.10	8.00	7.50
2011	7.70	8.70	8.30
2016	8.70	9.80	9.30
2021	10.20	11.30	10.70
2026	11.80	13.10	12.14

Source: Office of the Registrar General of India quoted by NSID, Jan., 2008: 2.

Table 1.7: Life Expectancy in India

Census Year	*Gender*	*Life Expectancy*
1951	M	32.5
	F	31.7
1961	M	41.9
	F	40.6
1971	M	47.1
	F	45.6
1981	M	54.8
	F	52.0
1991	M	60.8
	F	61.7
2001	M	62.4
	F	63.4
2011	M	66.12
	F	68.22

Source: Census of India, New Delhi.

The life expectancy, which was around 29 years in 1947, is now closer to 68 years. The same is expected to increase to 71 years by 2026 (NISD, 2008:1). The life expectancy for India in 2019 was 69.50 years. The current life expectancy for India in 2020 is 69.73 years.

The life expectancy at birth during 2009-2013 was 69.3 for females as against 65.8 years for males.

Further, between 2001 and 2026, due to decling fertility, the proportion of population aged under 15 years is projected to decline from 35.4 to 23.4 per cent; the proportion of the middle (15-59 years) and the older ages (60 years and above) are set to increase considerably. With the declining fertility, coupled with the increase in life expectancy, the number of older persons in the population is expected to increase by more than double from 76 million in 2001 to 173 million in 2026-an increase in their share to the total population from 7.4 to 12.4 percent. The proportion of population in the working age group (15-59 years) is expected to rise from 57.7 percent in 2001 to 64.3 percent in 2026. The sex-ratio of the total population (females per 1000 males) is expected to decrease (i.e. become less feminine) from 933 in 2001 to 930 during 2026. However, on the contrary, sex ratio among the 60+ is expected to rise i.e. older women will outnumber their male counterparts. (NISD, 2008:1).

An examination of increasing life expectancy at all ages indicates that these will be increase longevity and longevity of female in older age group will create many familial and socio-economic problems of adjustment.

It is important to mention here the socio-economic characteristics of senior citizens in India.

Even after 73 years of independence, a large number of Indians are illiterate. In this era of globalization there is a great urgency to bring about total literacy in the country within a few years. Undoubtedly education promotes social safety nets. It is an important social infrastructure. Kirit S. Parikh (2002: 103) has rightly mentioned that, "the importance of education can not be overstressed. Illiteracy is a prison and education frees one from that prison. It increases people's awareness of opportunities for advancement and imparts the ability to seize them. Self-help is easier for an educated person. Knowledge of one's rights empowers a person and a literate person is able to acquire that knowledge. Literacy is thus the first step to empowerment." In as much as the scopes of opportunities have widened with globalization, it has increased the importance of education.

Table below shows the literacy levels in the general population and the aged of India, by sex and place of residence.

Table 1.8: Literacy Rate (%) Among All Ages and Elderly Persons

Year	*Males (All ages)*			*Females (All ages)*			*Males (60+)*			*Females (60+)*		
	Total	*Rural*	*Urban*	*Total*	*Rural*	*Urban*	*Total*	*Rural*	*Urban*	*Total*	*Rural*	*Urban*
1961	34.46	29.09	57.49	12.96	8.55	34.51	29.18	24.36	55.89	4.30	2.28	15.82
1981	46.89	40.79	65.83	24.82	17.96	47.82	34.79	28.74	61.03	7.89	4.44	21.82
1991	52.75	47.07	68.76	32.17	24.85	53.85	40.62	33.65	65.97	12.68	7.51	30.76

Sources: Census of India, 1961, 1981, 1991.

Note: The Census of India, 1971 had no data presented separately on the literacy of elderly people.

It is obvious from the above table that there is a relatively lower level of literacy among the aged persons. Female elderly are much more illiterate than their male counterparts. The urban elderly are more literate than the rural elderly. There has been an increase in literacy among both elderly males and females between 1961 and 2011, although by 2011, it was 59.1% among males and 28.5% among females. Still proportion of literate elderly is low. 'It is true that the present literacy levels among the elderly are pretty low, the future elderly are expected to be more literate and will be demanding more from the government for social security and other financial benefits.' (Rajan I.S. et.al., 1999).

The marital relationship plays a crucial support function in older people's lives, especially men's. As parental and employment / work responsibilities decline, having a spouse provides built-in companionship. The marital status data on the elderly population shows a fairly large proportion of them being widow (see table 1.9). Due to higher life expectancy at birth, the tendency for women to marry men older than themselves and death during work or death due to other reasons like accidents or war etc., are the three main reasons for increasing proportion of widowed women among the aged. One more reason for this gender disparity in widowhood may be that whereas widowed men often remarry, the widowed women cannot often due to social taboos, or non-availability of suitable spouse or for her own familial reasons. The quality of life is lowered for many Indian women because of widowhood (Parikh Kirit S., 2002). Elderly widows are the worst victims of abuse and neglect in the family.

There is an urgent need to empower women economically. Though, recently government has changed the inheritance laws to provide the women equal right to land and property, yet the traditional social laws still prevail.

Table 1.9: Marital Status of Elderly-India 2011

Age (years)	*Sex*	*Never Married*	*Married*	*Widow*	*Divorced/ Separated*
60+	Males	2.9	82.1	14.6	0.4
	Females	2.0	49.6	47.8	0.5
70-79	Males	2.2	78.3	19.1	0.4
	females	1.6	37.1	60.8	0.4
80+	Males	7.5	62.0	30.1	0.4
	Females	4.6	26.1	69.0	0.4

Source: Census of India, 2011.

One of the major problems of the Indian elderly is generally the low economic status. It is rightly observed that, 'the predominantly rural character accompanied with least proportion of population in wage and salaried employment affected by compulsory retirement ages, allows persons to be in work till they are able to do so. And in case of self employment, economic necessity forces many to continue working as long as they are able, though perhaps at a reduced pace' (Rajan S. et.al., 1999). At the same time, and contrary wise, the labour force participation of the older persons has declined over the last decades. (See table below) And, the main causative factors would appear to be the shrinkage of work and employment opportunities and to a growing extent as a result of the policy of globalization, such as the massive displacement in certain traditional sectors, e.g. household industry and agriculture labour.

Table 1.10: Trends in Labour Force Participation (65+). (India)

1950	*1975*	*2000*	*2025*	*2050*
44.1	41.1	34.8	32.1	29.6

Note: The labour force participation rate consists of the economically active population in a particular age group as a percentage of the total population of that same age group. The active population (or labour force) is defined as the sum of people in employment and unemployed people seeking employment.

Source: United Nations, "World Population Ageing 1950-2050, "Population Division, Department of Economic and Social Affairs, 2002.

The working age population in India is about 59 percent now; it will rise to 64.3 percent of 2025 and then expected to fall to 59.7 percent in 2050. The expected increase in old-age dependency is from about 8.1% now to 12.2 percent in 2025 and 22.6 percent in 2050. (See table no.1.11)

Table 1.11: Trends in Proportion of Working Age Population (15 – 59 years), Total Dependency Ratio, Old-Age Dependency Ratio – India.

Trends	*1950*	*1975*	*2000*	*2025*	*2050*
Proportion Working Age Population (15-59 years)	55.5	54.0	58.9	64.3	59.7
Total Dependency Ratio*	73.2	77.4	62.5	46.1	52.6
Old-Age Dependency Ratio**	5.8	6.8	8.1	12.2	22.6

* The total dependency ratio is the number of persons under age 15 years plus persons aged 65 years or older per 100 persons in the category of 15 to 64 years. It is the sum of the youth dependency ratio and the old-age dependency ratio.

** The old-age dependency ratio is the number of persons 65 years and over per 100 persons 15 to 64 years.

Source: United Nations, "World Population Aging 1950-2050" Population Division, Department of Economics and Social Affairs, 2002.

India is in the intermediate stage of ageing process as the median age; at present is less than 30. The trends in Ageing Index and also in Median Age show rapid increase in near future, which may lead to compelling demands for changes in the way societal resources are shared between generations (Rakesh Mohan, 2004: 302).

Table 1.12: Trends in Ageing Index and Median Age

Trends	1950	1975	2000	2025	2050
Ageing Index*	14.4	15.6	22.7	53.6	105.0
Median Age**	20.4	20.0	23.7	31.3	38.0

* The ageing index is calculated as the number of persons under age of 15 years.

** The median age is the age, which divides the population into two equal halves. It can therefore reflect the ageing phenomenon as it determines whether a given population is young or old (Rajan et.al., p. 28-29).

Source: United Nations, "World Population Ageing 1950-2050", Ibid.

Weakening of the Support System

Ageing has never been a problem in traditional Indian Society. Historically, growing up has been a symbol of grace and dignity. Old people had been on the social agenda since ancient times within a framework social economy where economic and other needs of the old remained a moral responsibility of family, Kin and Community.

A paradoxical situation is developing in India. If, on the one hand, the population of the aged has increased over the successive decades, on the other hand, due to several socio-economic factors the so-called Indian Welfare Society is collapsing. At the same time the traditional family / community based support system for the ageds have weakened.

Indeed, not unlike 'desertion' of women, desertion of old parents has shot up as a serious problem to the extent that some states in India (e.g. Himanchal Pradesh) have enacted a law extending the scope of the provision of maintenance of deserted women by their husbands, to parents abandoned by their sons. The government of Maharastra and to some extent Goa too, has prepared a Bill on a similar line. The right of parents without any means to be supported by their children having sufficient means has been recognised by section 125 (1) (d) of the Code of Criminal Procedure 1973, and section 20 (3) of the Hindu Adoption and Maintenance Act, 1956. Another heir (s) law in the offing is to deprive the negligent of their parents, of any share in the ancestral property. Evidently, the problem is getting more acute in the regions and sections of the society prone to migration in search of work and employment. Apparently, the problem must be more acute among the asset-less labouring class who cannot earn beyond their own survival. No doubt, the syndrome manifests among the middle classes also where the tendency of neglect of the old parents may be more due to 'selfishness'.

Concept of Elder Abuse And Neglect

Of the various problems faced by the older adults, the most serious one which has emerged in the changing scenario of the socio-economic order today is the problem of elder abuse and neglect. It is a serious widespread social problem, affecting millions of elderly people across the country. It is largely hidden under the shroud of secrecy, and, as a result, it is grossly under-reported. It raises many complex ethical, legal and clinical questions.

What is Elder Abuse ?

The abuse of older people by family members dates back to ancient times. But their are others who says that it is a relatively recent occurrence in contemporary society due to processes of modernization. According to Kosberg and Garcia (1995) socio economic problems stemming from modernization and industralization were the most commonly cited reasons for increased abuse. This is due primarily to the acute juxtaposition of traditional orientations and modern instrumental value bases.

There is no consensus as to how elder abuse should be defined (see different views of scholars like Block and Sinnott (1979), Lau and Kosberg (1979), Douglass et.al. (1980), etc.). To a great extent, abuse is culture – specific and also specific to time and place. There is also a class dimension to this form of abuse (Nayar P.K.B., 2004). It is generally agreed that abuse of older people is either an act of commission or of omission (in which case it is usually described as "neglect'), and that it may be either intentional or unintentional. The abuse may be of a physical nature, it may be psychological (involving emotional or verbal aggression), or it may involve financial or other material maltreatment. Regardless of the type of abuse, it will certainly result in unnecessary suffering, injury or pain, the loss or violation of human rights, and a decreased quality of life for the older person. (Hudson, M.F.:1991, in WRVH,: 126)

It is a fact that universally applicable definition of elder abuse is not available. Stones, MJ (1995) discusses the three approaches toward meaning and definition of elder abuse and neglect which differ in terms of their intent and also regarding their products the approaches are *connotative* (attempts *to* specify the full meaning), *structural* (refers to the criteria used to evaluate abuse) and *denotative* (example of abuse). According to him abuse is, "a misdemeanor against acknowledged standards by someone a senior has reason to trust". (referred by Nahmiash, Daphne, 2002: 22-23)

In its common usage, elder abuse is an all-inclusive term representing all types of mistreatment or abusive behavior toward older adults. This mistreatment can be an act of commission (abuse) or emission (neglect) intentional or unintentional, and of one or more types: physical, psychological (or emotional) or financial abuse and neglect that results in unnecessary suffering, injury, loss or violation of human rights, and decreased quality of life (Hudson, 1991). Whether a behavior is labeled as a abusive, neglectful, or exploitative may depend on its frequency, duration, intensity, severity, consequences and cultural context.

Elder abuse is the mistreatment or neglect of an older person usually by a relative or other care giver (Office of the Fayette Common Wealth's Attorney 2008). It results in harm or loss to an older person. Elder abuse can be defined as "a single or repeated act or lack of appropriate action, occurring within any relationship where there is an act of trust which causes harm or distress to an older person" (WHO 1980).

The National Research Council defines elder mistreatment as intentional actions that cause harm (whether or not harm was intended) or create a serious risk of harm to an older adult by a caregiver or other person who stands in a trust relationship to the elder, or failure by a caregiver to satisfy the elder's basic needs or to protect the elder from harm (Bonnie, 2003).

In a country report for World Health Organization, the problem of elder abuse in India was discussed through the techniques of focus group discussions. This study was designed with the overall aims of defining, the symptoms of elder abuse, the spreading of awareness about its existence among the primary health care workers and also developed a strategy for its prevention the participant did not link violence to the elder abuse. They however did acknowledge the existence of "maltreatment", "neglect" and "disrespect" within their society and community (Soneja, 2002).

There is no consensus regarding the definition of elder abuse and efforts to define this term accurately have met with little success. With some of these definitions there seems to be a drive to include all forms of troubled interpersonal relationships under the rubric of violence and abuse. T.F. Johnson (1986), in a comprehensive review of definition of elder abuse, provides an example of this problem. She noted that definitions often include psychological mistreatment of the elderly. "This type of abuse has been seen as including such behavior as making the old person feel ashamed of his or her behavior/ridiculing the elder, shouting at him or her, or interfering with the old person's decision making regarding his or her own activities. In contrast, the term abuse has generally been limited to actions that are much further beyond the range of normal human relationships such as physical violence that results in injury, or is intended to result in injury." (Hudson, M.F. & T.F. Johnson, 1986)

Rather than attempting to resolve the debate over the definition of elder abuse, some of social scientists have focused on domestic violence against the elderly persons. Straus, Gelles, and Steinmetz (1980) have employed the concept of violence to explain the elderly abuse. To them "an act carried out with the intention or perceived intention of causing physical pain or injury to another persons." In this sense they used the term domestic violence against the elderly and elder abuse interchangeably.

The definition developed by Action on Elder Abuse in the United Kingdom (1995: 11) and adopted by the International Network for the Prevention of Elder Abuse states that," Elder abuse is a single or repeated act, or lack of appropriate action, occuring within any relationship where there is an expectation or distress to an older person" (Quoted by WRVH: 126-127).

Kosberg and Garcia (1995) has pointed out that this definition of elder abuse has been heavily influenced by the work done in Canada, the United Kingdom and the United States. Studies conducted in China (Hong Kong SAR), Finland, Greece, India, Ireland, Israel, Norway, Poland and South Africa have approached the topic in distinctly different ways. The authors has mentioned some of the customs and culturally accepted practices in India and Africa too, which world considered cruel for example forced levirate marriages, expulsion of childless widows from their homes and accusations of witchcraft to older woman.

Elder abuse and neglect has not deserved the attention of social scientist and social planners which it ought to have. The World Report on Violence and Health, (Oct. 2002), pointed out that, "abuse of the elderly is one of the most hidden faces of violence; up to 6% of the elderly report having been abused. The United Nations International Plan of Action adopted by all countries in Madrid, April 2002, recognized the importance of elder abuse and put it in the framework of the Universal Human Rights. Elder abuse is still a 'hidden' phenomenon in many countries. Thus, the issue of bringing it 'forward' and legimitizing it as a social problem is of utmost importance. (Ariela Lowenstein, 2006: 6-7)

Tina A. Ambani (2006:4), President, Harmony Foundation, Mumbai has rightly pointed out that elder abuse is an unpleasant malady of modern day society. It is universal and crosses all geographic, socio-economic, racial and ethnic barriers. Since it is often hidden in the shroud of family secrecy, it is grossly under reported. Elder abuse often goes unreported on account of several factors, including-

* It being a family affair,
* Hesitation to lable a child or spouse as an abuser,
* Embarrassment,
* Fear of being labeled demented or incapable,
* Fear of retaliation,
* Fear of being removed from home is worse than the abuse,

* Lack of social and familial awareness,
* Isolation of some groups of older persons, especially migrants,
* Lack of awareness concerning whom to report,
* Belief among the elders that they are the cause of the problem, and
* Belief among the elders that they are being paid back for their earlier abuse of a spouse or child. (Lowenstein, Doron and Winterstein, 2004)

According to Devi Prasad (1996:2), elder abuse does constitute a separate category of abuse requiring special attention for three important reasons. They are:

* The elderly constitute a vulnerable group, especially those over 75 years become more and more vulnerable to abuse and neglect. This is more so because of their devalued social status and dependency on family, which increases as they advance in age.
* It is learned from the many preliminary studies both in India and in the West, that elder abuse though not widely acknowledged, exists. It is estimated that in USA alone, around 5,00,000 to 2.5 million elderly are subjected to physical violence annually (U.S. Select Committee, 1981). A few Indian studies also gave strong indication as to the existence of maltreatment of elderly in the family context (Sivaraju, 2003, Srinivas and Vijayalaxmi, 2001; Rao, 1995; Usharani, 1989; Vijayakumar, 1991; Vlassoff and Vlassoff, 1980).
* The maltreatment of the elderly significantly undermines the quality of their life and may have a profound effect on the moral fibre of the society.

Types of Elder Abuse

Elder abuse can be of various forms such as physical, psychological/ emotional, sexual and financial abuse. It can also simply reflect intentional or unintentional neglect. Several types of mistreatment may occur simultaneously. The personal losses associated with the abuse can be devastating and include the loss of independence, home, life savings, health, dignity and security. Victims of abuse have been shown to have shorter expectancy than non-abused older people.

O'Malley et al. (1983), simplified the conditions of abuse to 'physical, psychological or financial injury' and defined neglect as the 'failure of a caretaker to intervene to resolve a significant need despite awareness of available resources.' WHO (2002) in their one of the study concluded that older people perceive abuse as neglect, isolation, abandonment and social exclusion; violation of human, legal and medical rights; and deprivation of choices, decisions, status, finances and respect.

Hooyman and Kiyak (1988: 281) has pointed out five commonly defined types of maltreatment, often together referred to as abuse, are:

Physical or sexual abuse: Malnutrition or injuries such as bruises, welts, sprains, dislocations, abrasions, or lacerations.

Psychological abuse: Verbal assault, threat, fear or isolation.

Exploitation: Theft or misuse of the person or the person's money or property for another person's profit or advantage.

Medical Abuse: Withholding or improper administration of needed medications, or withholding of aids such as dentures, glasses, or hearing aids.

Neglect: Conduct by the vulnerable adults or others resulting in the deprivation of care necessary to maintain physical and mental health.

With large-scale migration of the young from rural to urban centers as well as to other countries in search of financially secure future, the problem of neglect is further intensified, and the elderly are left behind to fend for themselves. This is a common type of abuse in India (Nayar, PKB, 2004).

The National Centre on Elder Abuse (NCEA, 1998) defines seven different types of elder abuse: physical abuse, sexual abuse, emotional abuse, financial exploitation, neglect, abandonment, and self-neglect.

Physical Abuse: Use of physical force that may result in bodily injury, physical pain, or impairment.

Sexual Abuse: Infliction of anguish, pain or distress through verbal or non-verbal acts.

Financial/Material Exploitation: Illegal or improper use of an elder's funds, property or assets.

Neglect: The refusal or failure to fulfill any part of a person's obligations or duties to an elderly person.

Abandonment: The desertion of an elderly person by an individual who has physical custody of the elder or by a person who has assumed responsibility for providing care to the elder.

Self-Neglect: When an adult refuses vital services necessary to maintain health and welfare.

As regard to the most prevalent pattern of elder abuse scholars like Lau and Kosberg, 1979; Pillemer and Finkelhor, 1988 have mentioned physical violence as the most widespread form of maltreatment, whereas others like Steur and Austin, 1980; Wolf and Others, 1986 revealed neglect and financial exploitation as a significant form of abuse of the elderly. Several studies (Block and Sinnott, 1979; Rao, 1995; Wolf and Others, 1986 etc.) found psychological abuse as the most prevalent pattern of elder abuse. Recent Indian studies (Devi Prasad, 2008; Avataramu, 2008; A.K. Joshi, 2005; Srinivas, 2004) also indicated a similar trend.

Precipitants of Elder Abuse and Neglect

Apart from the reasons responsible for elder abuse, social scientist have focused their attention on direct or indirect precipitant factors which are responsible for hidden violence and abuse against the elders in the family (Thomas Joseph, 2001). These factors are divided into two types:

- **Direct Precipitant**: There are five major factors related to domestic violence which are also related to elder abuse. There are (1) Intra- individual dynamics (2) Intergenerational transmission of violent behavior ("Cycle of Violence") (3) Inequitable levels of dependency between abuser and abused (4) Social Isolation (5) External Stress.

- **Intra-individual dynamics:** This view point lays blame on some pathological characteristics of the abuser, usually mental illness of some kind. Research by Wolf (1998) found a considerable degree of mental illness among elder abusers; 31% were reported to have a history of psychiatric illness. Pillemer also found abusers to be much more likely to have a history of psychiatric hospitalization than a non-abuse control group. Some of the other researchers hold the view that alcoholic, frustrated, and angry adults are mainly responsible for abusing the elders.
- **Intergenerational transmission of violent behavior:** Some of the researches have pointed out that some families have the tradition of violence. The children and adults learned this trait in the family and in return they have become violent to the elders as well.
- **Inequitable levels of dependency between abuser and abused:** Another commonly cited factor in the elder abuse literature is the resentment generated by the dependency of an older person on a caretaker. This view has developed in large part from gerontological research on the strains of family care giving to elderly relatives.

Thus, Davidson (1979) tied abuse directly to the "crises" created by the needs of an elderly parent for care. Steinmetz (1988) argued that families undergo "generational inversions" in which the elderly person becomes dependent on his or her children for financial, physical, and/or emotional support, leading to severe stress on the part of the caregiver. As the costs of the relationship grow for the caregiver, and the rewards diminish, the exchange becomes perceived as unfair, if the care taker feels unable to escape the situation, he or she may then become abusive.

- **Social Isolation:** Social isolation has been found to be characteristic of families in which other forms of domestic violence occurs. This is probably because behaviors that are considered to be illegitimate tend to be hidden. Detection of family violence can result in informal sanctions from friends, kin and neighbors, and formal sanctions from police and the courts. Thus, all forms of family violence are likely to be less frequent in families that have friends or relatives who live nearby. Isolation often leads to elder abuse.

- **External Stress:** Some of the researchers have found positive relationship between external stress at differentiated from the stress that results from interpersonal relationships in the family. Unemployment, poor economic condition, loss of job etc. are the contributory factors which are to be elder abuse.

Indirect Precipitant: Some of the researchers have focused on the problem of elder abuse through the prism of indirect precipitant. These researches the family relations mainly the parent, child relationships, marital relationship among the spouses, incongruence of values, status transitions may contribute to elder abuse and neglect.

In a study Acierno (2009) has found 11 percent of cognitively intact older adults become victims of elder mistreatment. Among cognitively intact older adults. a nationally representative sample revealed that the prevalence of older mistreatment was 4.6 percent for psychological mistreatment, 1.6 percent for physical abuse, 0.6 percent for sexual abuse, 5.1 percent for neglect, and 5.2 percent for financial abuse. Elder mistreatment among older adults with cognitive impairment appears to be markedly higher. Wiglesworth, et.al. (2010) in their study found that in a convenience sample of adults with cognitive sample of adults with cognitive impairment and their caregivers, 47.3 percent of adults with cognitive impairment were found to have experienced elder mistreatment. Specially, 88.5 percent experienced psychological abuse, 19.7 percent experienced physical abuse, and 29.5 percent experienced neglect.

The characteristics of the older adults that have been shown to be associated with a greater risk of elder mistreatment (Kerry Burnight and Laura Mosqueda, 2011:5-6) include: cognitive impairment (Wiglesworth et al. 2010); social isolation (Lachs et al., 1994); lower household income, need for ADL assistance (Acierno, 2009), and previous traumatic event (Acierno, 2009). A shared living arrangement is a major risk factor for elder mistreatment (Lachs et al. 1997). Perpetrator risk factors include family relation (Lachs et al. 1994), substance abuse (Antetzberger et al., 1994), mental illness (Pulmer and Gurland, 1996), dependency (Pillemer & Finkelhor, 1989), unemployment (Acierno, 2009), criminal history (Klien et al., 2008).

Theoretical Approaches

The phenomenon of elder abuse is quite complex and rapidly changing in the differential ecological and socio-cultural milieu. Various curative theories have been advanced to explain the phenomenon but no one single theory is sufficient to explain the phenomenon of elder abuse and neglect in its totality. There is considerable overlapping in these theoretical models. It is rightly pointed out that, "Elder mistreatment inquiry is a relative newcomer to the family violence arena and its stockpile of empirically-based knowledge lacks a theoretical framework within which to understand its multiple manifestations." (Kerry Burnight and Laura Mosqueda, (2011:1-2).

Researchers have offered various theoretical explanation of why elder abuse occurs: an overburdened care giver (situational model), a dependent elder or perpetrator (exchange theory), a mental emotionally disturbed perpetrator (psychopathology), and a childhood of abuse and neglect (social learning theory). Others have criticized the emphasis on individual traits. They propose that structural forces such as the imbalance of power within relationships (feminist theory) or the marginalization of elders within society (political economic theory) have created conditions that lead to conflict and violence.

Some of the researchers have used system model to explain the phenomenon of elder abuse. The study of Daphne Nahmiash (2002) on "Powerlessness and Abuse and Neglect of Older Adults", is a qualitative study which addresses the interacting relationship between the environmental context of care giving and abuse and neglect of older adults. This study demonstrate that violence is produced by complex interacting systems and significant events, that impact on the life courses of some older adults and some caregivers leading them into powerless positions and resulting in abuse and neglect.

A schematic presentation of system model (Nahmiash, Daphne, 2002: 41) for the study of powerlessness, abuse and neglect is as follows:

A Systemic Model of how abuse and neglect interact with diverse contexts and factors

MACRO SYSTEM Early Construction of identity as caregiver, protector, perfect wife/mother, Learned gender and culture roles and attitudes
EXO SYSTEM Oppressive measures and policies in health and social service systems and criminal justice systems. Lack of choices, negative societal attitudes and culture attitudes (ageism). Lack of resources and information.
MESO SYSTEM Present social and economic and culture context isolation: living arrangements, family secrets, poor health, family violence/conflicts.
MICRO SYSTEMS Co-dependent relationships (often related to substance abuse).
POWERLESSNESS Fear, aloneness, "seeing a black world", unable to defend themselves. Lack of control, self blame
ABUSE AND NEGLECT Loss of control Loss of identity Loss of space, home, land

Source: Journal of Elder Abuse & Neglect, 14 (1)

Guided by the empirical findings of several studies, a number of theoretical approaches have been applied to the etiology of elder abuse. Kerry Burnight and Laura Mosqueda (2011: 6-7) has mentioned following theoretical approaches that have been used in trying to understand elder mistreatment.

Intrapersonal Theory

- Social Learning Theory

Interpersonal Theory

- Caregiver Stress Theory
- Social Exchange Theory
- Dyadic Discord Theory

Socio-cultural Theories

- Power and Control Theory

Multisystemic Theories

- Ecological Theory
- Socio-cultural Context

Psychopathological Model: It emphasizes the psychological problems of the abusers. Drug and alcohol are considered to be mainly responsible for the abusers mistreatment of the elders. The abuser may be actually mentally ill or suffer from unresolved emotional or psychiatric problems that result in violent sociopathic behaviours directed against the elderly family members. This theoretical model is anchored in the psychological and behavioural problems of the abuser and the helpless elder becomes the worst sufferer. (Sengstock M, Liang J 1982).

The Social Learning Theory: The basic assumption of this theory which was developed in the child maltreatment literature, is that, violence is a learned behaviour passed on through the generations (Kerry Burnight and Laura Mosqueda, 2011:9). Social Learning Theory (Bandura, 1973) is an explanation that has been applied to elder mistreatment that has been variously called the Cycle of Violence Theory, Social Learning Theory and the intergenerational Transmission of Violence Theory.

This model suggests that abusive adults were abused as children (Hickey T, Douglass, R. 1981). In some families domestic violence is a learnt behaviour when the parental role model is abusive (Sengstock M, Barretts, S. Graham R. 1982). Once the abused child reaches adulthood, the resource power balance has shifted to the child, and he may see the remain for the suffering endured as a child by abusing the aged parent. Korbin and Colleagues (1995) in their study found that those who mistreat children were significantly more likely to have experienced more severe forms of violence as children, such as being hit with a fist, bitten, kicked, and threatened with a gun or knife.

To examine the salience of learned violence, Wolf and Pillemere (1989) compared abused seniors (their offspring were the perpetrators) and non-abused seniors in their responses about their method of punishment and found no significant differences.

Caregiver Stress Theory: It is said that, "Abuse of the elder is precipitated by stress" (McLaughlin et al., 1980). In this theory the elderly victim is viewed as dependent on the caregiver who becomes overwhelmed, frustrated, and abusive because of the continuous caretaking needs of the infirm care recipient (Kerry Burnight and Laura Mosqueda, 2011:7) this theory posits that elder mistreatment occurs when an adult is not able to manage his or her caregiving responsibilities (Wolf, 2000).

Situational Stress Model: According to this model duties and responsibilities that are associated with providing personal care for an elderly parent may place overwhelming demands on the adult child caregiver. The adult child may have to give up this previous life style including entertainment, social relationships, and possibly his job, to be home to care for the elderly parent (Steur J, Austin E. 1980). It is wothmentioning here that, empirical research examining the relationship between stress and elder mistreatment has shown that while stress is linked with mistreatment in some manner, and may be an intensifier of potential mistreatment; it is not clear predictor (Hudsun, 1986).

Other stress factor may include lack of finances to provide proper care in adequate housing or overcrowding, lack of support from other family members, illness or physical impairment of the adult children themselves and general lack of awareness that services are available to help cope with those stresses.

Ecological Theory

As a way of accommodating the complexity and multiplicity of factors and theories associated with elder abuse, researchers such as Schiamberg and Gans 1999 and Carp 1999 are turning to an "ecological" model, first applied to child abuse (Garbarino and Crouter, 1978; Garbarino and Kostelny, 1992) and, more recently, to intimate partner violence (Chalk and King, 1998). In this model, violence results from individual, interpersonal and societal factors. The advantage of this model is that it allows elder abuse to be linked to broader social issues.

This theory lays stress on the broader contextual frame within which elder abuse occurs rather than concentrating on individual characteristics of elderly victims and their abusers. The increasing rates of elder abuse by adult children are an instance of violence between intimates with significant implications for families. Given the complexity of elder abuse by adult children and the facts that relevant risk factors for such abuse are related to individuals (i.e. adult child as care giver and older adults as care recipient), the socio/cultural context of individuals, and the interactions between person and context, an ecological prospective provides an effective framework for explaining elder abuse as an inter-generational family problem. (Kosberg & Nahmias, 1996).

This theory was developed to try to capture a number of potential causes and organize them into groups (Bronfenbrenner, 1979). Parra-Cardone and colleagues (2007) used an ecological model to bring to light variables to consider in the study of Latino families affected by elder abuse. Kerry Burnight and Laura Mosqueda (2011:18) has presented an ecological model of etiology of elder mistreatment by a figure below which depict that in Ecological theory, cultural and societal beliefs are grouped in the outer ring of concentric circles. Variables in the macrosystem are: age and gender inequality, societal aggression norms. In the exosystem variables are economic environment, integration into the community. Variables in the microsystem variables are individual and family characteristics. In the ontogenetic system, variables include physiology, affect and behaviour.

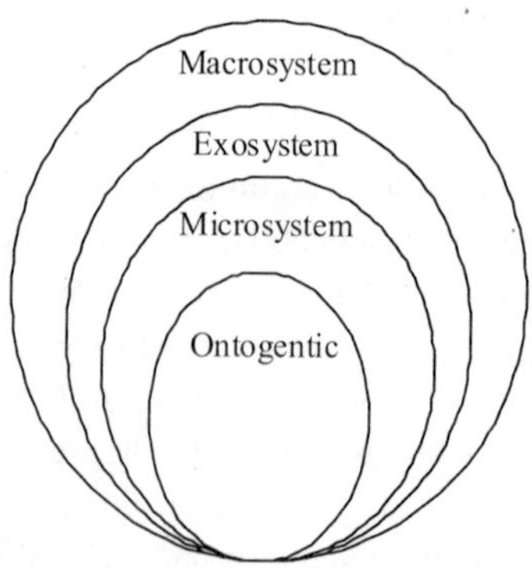

This approach utilizes an ecological, bi-focal model for elder abuse by adult children, focusing simultaneously on the adult child and the aging parent as a familial dyad. This model posits the essential and critical role of the intergenerational relationship between an adult child and an aging parent, over the life course, as a primary basis for both understanding elder abuse. (Schiamberg & Gans, 1999, 2000, 2003; Bronfenbrenner, 1979, 1986, 1997, Elder & Johnson, 2002; Elder, Johnson & Cronsoe, 2003).It helps identify variables for inclusion but does not constitute any particular set of predictions to test so when using ecological models (Kerry burnight and Laura Mosqueda, 2011:17).

Exchange Theory: This theory is developed by sociologist George Casper Homans in 1950's. It focuses on inter-personal relationship and is predicated on a neo-economic rationale that contents that people seek to maximize regards and satisfaction while minimizing cost in all interaction. (Cook 1992). In gerontology such an approach looks at the way older people are perceived and how such a view affects their interaction with others. Patterns of support, intergenerational interaction, and historical changes in opportunities structure and the perceived value of elderly are frequently analyzed by using an exchange model (Antonucci, 1990; Lee, 1988; Riley, Kahn & Foner, 1994; Whitebeck, Hoyt & Huck, 1994). This theory explains interactions between people as a process of negotiated exchanges. Social behaviour is considered an exchange of material and non-material goods. Material goods include things like money, living arrangements, inheritance, and non-material goods include approval, presige, etc. Persons that receive a lot from others are under pressure to give much to them in return (Homans, 1958).

This theoretical model explains the phenomenon of elder abuse on the basis of unequal exchange values among the family members as the care-giver and elder as the care recipient. The elders because of loss of income, loss of job, and physical debility are reduced to the status of unequal partners in the inter-personal relationships of the family. The family members expect more benefits from the elders who are not in a position to provide such benefits. This results into neglect, misbehaviour and abuse by the family members. (Homans, 1960, Walker, Martin & Jones, 1992).

Dependency Theory: This theoretical model lays emphasis that the increasing dependency of elders occur because of several situational changes during the old age such as death of spouse, physical disability, chronic diseases, inability to perform normal daily chores, loss of social status, fear of death etc. This results into over dependency on family members. The elders become helpless physically, socially, economically and psychologically. In such situation the care giver becomes the dictating factor and the recipient elder has to receive what is being given to them. Thus, dependency is the most important causative factor of the elder abuse. (Shankardas, MK (1997), Hudson (1986)).

Survey of Literature

Research in Gerontology is a rapidly developing area of study. Such studies have a wide ranging focus on many different facets of population ageing; problems of elders, their interpersonal relationship, their welfare and rehabilitation of schemes.

Amesur (1959) in his article "Welfare Services for the aged and infirm" has written that due to industrialization, urbanization and modernization the family organization is experiencing change which ultimately has created many problems for the elders. This organization of the joint family and the rise of nuclear family have created problems for the care of the elders. The rising individualism and self-centeredness among the young generation's elders have become most neglected members of the family.

Block & Sinnott (1979) has found that those elders who are physically and mentally ill, they are more likely to be neglect and abuse.

Finkelhor, D. (1980) has described elder abuse as the consequence of unequal distribution of power in the family. The elders become powerless and the younger generation because of their economic strength possesses relatively greater power. This leads to neglect and abuse of the elders. He has also emphasized that unemployment, economic stringency are responseful for the elder abuse. Those families which have distant relationship with friends, relatives and community members in such families elder abuse may occur in greater proportion.

Holt, Reinhart & Winston (1985) have defined elder abuse as the purposively designed activity of the family members which may be verbal abuse or else physical assault. They have stated that not providing meal to the elders, making misuse of the wealth of elders, desertion of the elders or threaten them to send them to old age home are the abuse of the elders by the family.

Pillemere & Wolf (1986) has stated that elder abuse is correlated with the rise in the aging population, population disorganization, economic uncertainty and decay of community feeling and decline of socio-cultural values. Intergenerational conflict is also responsible for elder abuse.

Finkelhor & Pillemer (1988) have studied the problem of elder abuse and violence in the family in relation to child abuse, wife battering etc. They have stated that the neglect and abuse in the family are the reflection of violence in the society against the powerless and weak groups in the society. Elders are physically disabled person and economically dependent upon other members in the family. Therefore there occurs tension in the family and the chances of elder abuse increases manifold in such situation. They are also of the opinions that elder abuse has got distinct characteristics of their own and therefore it should be treated as a separate category for scientific investigation.

Mildred D. Pajelow (1989) is of the opinion that the elder abuse has its origin in rapid population growth and poor mechanism to check the growth of population. Elder abuse is mostly found in the middle and lower middle class section of the population. According to him elder abuse is mostly visible in the form of psychological torture, economic exploitation and neglect rather than in the form of physical assault.

Glendenning (1997) has specified that elder abuse is intentional and voluntary behaviour to debase the elders whereas neglect is an act which happens unknowingly and providing harm to the elders. Abuse may be of different types such as physical, psychological, social etc. neglect done deliberately and to deprive the elders their rightful place in the family very serious problems of the elders.

Josheph Thomas (2001) has reported five reasons of elder abuse- interpersonal relationship, generational transfer of violent behaviour, dependency of elders, social isolation and external pressure.

John Baldock (2001) has opined that the physical debility of the elders and their dependency have made the old age a problematic situation. He is also of the opinion that the traditional society women were primarily responsible for the care of the elders but the apathy of woman towards family responsibility, their engagement of Job market, selfishness of younger generation and changes in the traditional value are responsible for the lack of family care of the elders, because in old age the elders become non-productive therefore treated as burden to the family.

Elsie Chau and Catherine So (2004) have studied the risk factors for elder abuse among Hong-Kong, Chinese families. It was found that the most common form of abuse was verbal abuse whereas physical abuse and violation of personal rights were relatively less common. There was no gender difference in the prevalence of elder abuse.

Morgan & Kunkel (2001) have reported that due to advance age elders become dependent upon their sons. As the load increased upon the care-taker the possibility of abuse against the elder also increases. sometimes those parents who have tortured the young one they retaliate against the old parents. Family environment is the source of mistreatment of the elders.

Sarah Lamb (2007) has stated that the changes in the family organization and the changing attitude of younger generation are mainly responsible for elder abuse and neglect. In such change atmosphere most of the elders prefer to live separately from their sons.

D'souza V (1971) has reported that due to changes in Indian social structure and family the problems of elders have increased. The status and role of the elders have changed. The status of the elder is defined more by their economic power rather than by their age and other achievement in life.

Soodan (1975) has studied elders in the city of Lucknow. It was found that the half of the elders were fully dependent upon their family and they had no income of their own. The study has underlined four major problems of the elders. These were economic problems, medical and health problems, status change and lack of facilities to utilize leisure time.

D 'Souza V (1982) has stated that the passing of peasant society into industrial society, the change of joint family system and the replacement by the nuclear family and rising individualism are mainly responsible for the deteriorating status of elders.

Bhatia, H.S. (1983) has studied the retired employ of the Udaipur city. He has found that no specific retirement plan was prepared by the employees after retirement. These elders were deprived of their previous income and found themselves very difficult situation. They became vulnerable to family neglect and abuse.

Desai, K.G. (1985) has found that in his study, most of the elders are living with their children or relatives and as such they were not feeling lonely and alienated but indirectly they were the neglected member of the family. Due to old age elders can not take part in the domestic duty. This leads to insecurity and loss of status to them.

Ranjan, R. (1986) has studied 100 male and female elders of Patna. He has found most of them were suffering from economic and health problems. Social isolation was found more among the male elders than among the female members. Moreover the study has noted that conservatism and rigidity among the elders are mainly responsible for elder's predicament.

Tayal, S. (1986) has found that the depression among the elders mainly the result of neglect by the family.

Kaur, Malikit, Grover, R.P. & Agarwal, K. (1987) have found that the younger generations feel that elders are unwanted burden. Their strain in the family leads to quarrel in the family.

Mishra, Saraswati (1987) has studied 300 retired government employees. This study suggests that the decline of status and loss of respect to elders are mainly due to disorganization of the joint family. The elders get alienated from the domestic chores which lead to loss of status.

Mahajan, A. (1987) has studied the economically deprived the elders of Haryana. He has found that 30 percent elders were given some supports by their family. While 70 percent were deserted by their family and there was none to take care of them. It has been found that physical inability and loss of income were mainly responsible for the neglect and desertion by the elders.

Nayar, P.K.B. (1987) is of the opinion that modernization, industrialization and urbanization occupational differentiation and rise of individualism or responsible for the changing the traditional values and declining status of the elders. Most of the members of younger generation do not pay as much respect to the elders as they used to do.

Sharma M.L. & Dak T.M. (1987) has analysed the problem of elders in contemporary society. He has stated that the traditional joint family elders were provided adequate security, respect and psychic gratification. But in contemporary India, western capitalism has changed the scenario. Individualism has risen, Migration of the younger generation increasing occupational mobility and changing life style have created problems for the elders.

Vijay Kumar & Suryanarayana (1989) have found that in rural areas extended family are extremely prevalent yet the elders do not possess that much power and authority as it used to prevail in traditional society. The traditional respect and security to elders have almost vanished. In recent times the elders are facing economic, psychic and health problems.

D'Souza, V. (1989) has found that the living conditions of the elders and changes in the structure of family have deep bearing upon the conditions of the elders. He is of the opinion that the increase in ageing population has adverse effect on the traditional prestige and security of the elders.

Natesan, H. (1990) has studied the elders above 60 years age in Coimbatore. His study is based on 50 male and 30 female elders. He has found that the major problems of elders are physical debility, sleeplessness, poor eyesight and illness. Those who are economically dependent elders, their major problems are lack of respect, social isolation, economic stringency, inability in obtaining proper job etc. This study has also revealed that economically dependent elders have relatively more problems than the self-dependent elders.

Mishra, S. (1991) has found that though in India elders and old age were never major problems. But in contemporary society changing social structure increase in individualism emphasis on materialistic values, negative attitudes of younger towards elders, retirement are the major contributing factors in the poor status of the elders.

Padmasree, V. (1991) has stated that elder abuse may be of two type-manifest abuse and latent abuse. Manifest abuse is direct incidence of violence and misbehaviour. Latent abuse is mainly threat to the elders, neglect of the elders and avoidance in the decision making in the family. She has noted that the major contributory factors of the abuse of the elders in the family are the poor economic status of the care taker, problems related to residence, physical disability of the elders and their dependency on others in the family.

Vijay Kumar, S. (1991) has studied the family life and living conditions of the elders in Chittoor district of Andhra Pradesh. His focus is mainly on changes in interpersonal relationship because of modernization and urbanization. He is of the view that in Indian society the problems of elders have arose because of disintegration of joint family and division of property. This adversely affected the social security to the elders which was provided by the family. The change in the institution of marriage has further weakened the hold of parents upon their younger generation which ultimately has increased the problems of elders.

Chaudhary, D.P. (1992) has stated that the problems of elders in India are-economic, physical, psychological, social and situational problems. Poor health of the elders and economic stringency are the other major problems which are contributed to the neglect and abuse of elders.

Nagesh, H.V. (1992) has studied the problems of loss of status and neglect to elders in the family situation. His study is also focused on the social security benefits and services available to elders.

Shah, V.P. (1993) has found that those old persons who had no property their own or no income were totally dependent upon their family, the behaviour of family members towards such old persons was generally unsatisfactory.

Dandekar, K. (1993, 1996) has studied old age homes in Maharashtra. He has found that lack of proper care, neglect and abuse meted out to the old persons in their homes were main reasons why they were staying in old age home. For them life in old age home was comparatively more satisfying than life in their family.

Mahajan, Amarjit and Madhurima (1995) have studied violence in the family including child abuse, women atrocities and elder abuse. They have specified that abuse is that behaviour which is intentionally meted out to others in order to inflict harm or injury.

Kasthoori, R. (1996) has studied the problems of elders in the city of Trivendrum, Kerala. It has been found that income status of the old aged person is correlated with their status in the family. The study has focused on the problems of social isolation and interpersonal relationship in their family.

Mukesh Ahuja (1996) has studied 190 widows of Jaipur. It has been found that most of them were victims of neglect by the family members. They are treated with abusive language threat, physical assault etc. These widows that they were physically assaulted in their in-laws family. Some of the widows reported that their son also physically assault them. Even the daughter-in-law beats them.

Chakravarthy, I. (1997) has analysed the ageing population in India and the changing socio-economic structure. He has stated that these changes are responsible for the abuse and low status of elders.

Kapur, P. (1997) has stated that elder abuse is a sensitive problem and it is on increase in India. Generally elder abuse is reflected in lack of family care, non fulfillment of basic needs such as food, clothes, shelter etc. Sometimes it is reflected in emotional detachment, verbal and physical assault. Sometimes the over indulgence of younger generation in social and economic responsibilities lead to neglect of elders.

Hussain, M.G. (1997) has found that increase in population of elders in India and disintegration of joint family have affected adversely the status of elders. The traditional joint family was helpful in solving the problems of elders. In recent times changes in the socio-economic values, migration of younger to outside native place in search of better economic opportunities are responsible for deteriorating status of parents. In urban areas the familial relationship has become very weak which has resulted into mistreatment and neglect of the elders.

Rajan, Mishra & Sarma (1999) have studied the problems of elders in Kerala and Tamilnadu. They have found that the married sons and daughters are living separately and do not pay attention to their old parents. Whatever care they receive is from their wife. The widows in the studies were not accepted by their progeny. For them neglect by the family members was very irritating and disturbing. The study has included some of the pension holder elderly women. They too found that younger generations do not pay as much respect to them as is expected. Further the study has made the survey of some elderly women living in old age home. These women stated that death of spouse, loss of property status was mainly responsible for their bad situation. Under very adverse circumstances they were forced to live in old age home.

Gangrade, K.D. (2000) has stated that the younger generations do not exhibit cordial and sympathetic relationships towards elders. He has found that the behaviour of younger generations towards elders is guided more by the social expectation around the discharge of responsibility towards elders rather than by respect and affection towards elders.

Jamuna, D. & Padmashree, V. (2000) have stated that the abuse and neglect of elders are likely to be more where the elders are physically disabled and economically dependent.

Rao, V.K., D.B. Prasad & Ch. Avataramu (2000) have found that abuse and neglect of family are largely dependent upon the nature of interaction of the family members with the elders. The negative attitude towards the elder is the resulted effect of interactive pattern which prevails in the family. This interactive pattern is created by the economic status, age, sex, educational status, and physical proximity of the family members. Moreover the life values and cultural patterning of the family governed the behaviour of family members towards elders.

Narayanswami, S. (2001) has analysed the legal and constitutional provisions for the safeguard of elders especially those elders who are the victims of hidden violence of the family. The old age pension scheme and the old age homes run by the governments as also the efforts of voluntary agency and NGO towards mitigating the miseries of elders have also been analysed.

Kuppuswamy, B. (2001) has emphasized that in the traditional agriculture based economy, the expertise and knowledge of elders were more in demand. These expertise and knowledge were transmitted from one generation to another not only in the socio-economic affair but also in the sphere of religious sacraments, the knowledge of the elders were of great use. However in recent times the expertise knowledge is being provided by the print media as well as by the electronic media. The younger generations feel that in contemporary technical society the elders knowledge is not much of use, therefore the respect of elders have decreased and the young generation looks towards elders with contempt and neglect.

Snehalata Tondon (2001) has studied the problems of elders in metropolitan Delhi with special reference to their needs and the governmental measures for the welfare of the elders. The study has concluded that the powerlessness of the older persons are responsible for the ill-treatment of the elders.

Gaur and Gaur (2001) have found that in the Urban Community because of industrialization, individualism has increased, members in the family have become self-centered and the little bothered about the family members. This disintegration two generation family instead of multigenerational family have contributed to the decline of status of elders.

Wadley, S.S. (2002) has reported that the joint family was great defense mechanism but this family system has disintegrated and therefore no one is taking the responsibility of care of the elders.

Himabindu, M. (2002) has based his study on the elderly women of villages in Andhra Pradesh. It has been emphasized that the generational conflict has contributed to the abuse and neglect of the elders.

Raju, S.S. (2002) have found that the problems of old age are the reflection of the conflict between traditional and western values. The younger generation experienced this conflict with great intensity. Therefore the communication between old and new breakdown and the status of elders is decline. The old age persons are facing the problem of neglect, mistreatment and discrimination.

Cohen, L. (2003) has reported that the due to disintegration of joint family, the problems of old aged persons have multiplied. There had been less respect and less cooperation available to old aged persons which are hindrances to their quality living.

Karlekar, M. (2003) has studied the problems of old aged persons. It was found that the increasing dependence of old age persons upon the younger ones is responsible for their neglect and abuse. The old ladies are more prone to neglect and abuse. In order to save the family prestige and also suffering from change, these old persons do not report their problems to other as a result mistreatment against them continues.

Rajan, I.S. and Sanjay Kumar (2003) have analysed the living conditions of the elders. The study has revealed that the most of the respondents live with their progeny. They have the family in domestic chores and also take care of the young child. Yet the relationships with the family members and with the younger generations are never very cordial.

Chakraborty, R.D. (2004) has stated that increasing deficiency is a physical power of the elders is mainly responsible for the neglect and abuse of the elders by those members of the family upon whom the elder is dependent. Old ladies are more victims of abuse than the male elders. One of the major problems in the reporting of the elder abuse is the fear and family prestige of the elders.

Kaushik, A. and Renu Sharma (2005) have reported that the informal mechanism of social defence such as joint family, Kinship, caste group have become weak because of modern sources of changes. This has created the problems for the elders. In addition the non-productivity of the elders and the physical debility are also responsible for mistreatment by the family.

Jamuna, D. (2005) has reported that the irritating and conservative nature of the elders coupled with the physical debility and economic dependency are responsible for their neglect and abuse by their family.

Joshi, A.K. (2006) has made a survey of 260 old aged persons in Varanasi. He has found that because of recent changes in the social and economic life, the traditional care mechanism of the elders in the family has also transformed considerably. The elders have no respect in their family or in their community. Most of the elders are neglected and experiencing socio-psycho problems. The cases of alienation, powerlessness, detachment and dependency are increasing in extreme cases the elders are deserting their family.

Bhat, N.V. (2006) has studied 150 elders of Shimoga district in Karnatak. The elders can live a relatively decent life until both of the spouse are alive when one of them become lonely, the problem of neglect and abuse aggravate.

Sandhu, J. and T. Arora (2006) have studied the 45 inmates of old age home in Amritsar. Most of these inmates show the shelter of old age home because they had strained relationship with their sons and daughter-in-law.

Mishra, A.K. and B.K. Mishra (2006) have stated that in modern society acquired achieved status on the basis of income and education along with rising individualism. The younger generations do not pay heed to the traditional values. Therefore the incidence of neglect and abuse are on increase.

Prabhabvathy Devi and Murugesan (2006: 2: 15-20) have studied the institutionalized elderly and functioning of Old Age Homes. They have found that in Old Age Homes the psychological and financial needs of the elderly are not adequately fulfilled.

Khan and Handa (2006: 2: 21-27) have analyzed case studies to identify the roots of elder abuse across different socio-economic groups and suggested interventions starting from the early childhood.

Singh, U.K. (2006) has studied the inmates of traditional shelter home of Varanasi. He has found that elders in difficult situations because of income sharing, property dispute, desertion by the family members have chosen to live in the traditional old age home in the city. Some of them were found to be very egoistic because they wanted to live an independent life without the interference of family members whereas some of the elders were on the verge of death and they were put in the traditional old age home especially meant for dying people.

Mallick, A. (2006) has studied the problems of old aged persons in Calcutta. He has stated that the old aged persons above 65 years are 10 percent (80 Lakhs) of the total population of the city. Most of the old aged persons have been deserted by their family mostly by the sons. He has found that the neglect and abuse of the elders are the resultant effects of the breakdown of the joint family, residential problem, selfishness and unsympathetic attitude of the elders, ideological differences are the main reasons. He has further found that the in comparison to physical assault most of the elders have to suffer verbal abuse, threat and abusive languages.

Rethi Devi, K. (2006) has found that elder abuse is mainly the reflection of increase in the population of elders and recent socio-economic changes. The status of the elders in the family depends upon the extent of the utility and activism on the part of the elders after retirement. Elders suffer from stress and hopelessness emerging in their attitude. Their dependency on the family also leads to domestic quarrels.

Patel, S. and S. Krishna (2007) have stated that elder abuse can be defined as deliberate action of the care-takers in the form of emotional injury and physical assault. He has also suggested the remedial measures for projecting interest of the elders.

Prabhavathy Devi, N. (2007) concluded that abuse of the elders is the single or repeated action of the family members to inflict emotional and physical injury to the elders. The inactivity of the elders and the apathy of the community are responsible for the abuse of the elders. This is also responsible for the under reporting of the elder abuse.

Mahajan, A. (2008) has found that the major cause of elder abuse directly and indirectly related with their dependency on other members in the family.

Joshi, AK & Meraj Hashmi (2009) have studied the problem of elder abuse in domestic setting in Varanasi. They have found that the elder abuse is mainly being done by the sons and daughters-in-law. Most of the cases of elder abuse is anchored in the ill-treatment regarding serving food and administration of medicine on time. Some of the elders in the study were inflicted physical injury. The suffering elders have reported the matter to friends, neighbours and relatives who have not been effective in providing remedial measures. In spite of these atrocities the elders in the study do not prefer to move to old age home. For them family is the place where they could get the solace and peace of mind than being away from the family.

Most of these studies are general in nature. There has been little attempt to develop theories and models of population ageing. Some of these studies are mainly demographic in nature which analyzes aggregate data. Micro studies of the elderly problems are far and few. More over research on neglect and abuse of elders are very scanty. The Indian situation presents another problem which relates to regional and ethnic diversities which make it difficult to arrive at general trends in the field of elder abuse in India. Some of the studies in India on elderly abuse are based on qualitative data which make it difficult to collate with other field studies.

Chapter - 2

Research Methodology

Origin of the Research Problem

In one of the document of the WHO/INPEA (2002:2) regarding history of elder abuse, it is mentioned that, "Societally hidden, but manifest in literature, child and wife abuse were the first to emerge. Both types of abuse were framed as family violence issues and were originally called baby battering and wife beating respectively. Eventually, the problem of elder abuse (which was initially called "granny battering") emerged." It remained a private matter, hidden from public view, till last quarter of 20th century. Karin Crawford and Janet Walker (2007: 113) has discussed about the range of words and phrases that have been used to describe the complex issues of vulnerability and abuse.

Biggs et al. (1995) provide a useful 'chronological development of terminology' in this area of elder abuse, which was developed by Karin Crawford and Janet Walker (2007: 113-114) as below:

Granny battering (Baker, 1975)

Elder abuse (O'Malley et al; 1979)

The battered elder syndrome (Block and Sinnott, 1979)

Elder mistreatment and vulnerable adults (Douglass et al. 1980)

Granny bashing (Eastman and Sutton, 1982)

Old age abuse (Eastman, 1984)

Inadequate care of elderly (Fulmer and O'Malley, 1987)

Granny abuse (Eastman, 1988)

Mis-care (Hocking, 1988)

Elder abuse (Dott, 1992)

The abuse of older people (Pritchard, 1995)

Adult protection (Dott, 2000)

Abuse of vulnerable adults (Dott, 2000; Pritchard, 2001)

Initially seen as a social welfare issue and subsequently a problem of aging, abuse of the elderly, like other forms of family violence, has developed into a major public health and criminal justice concern. (World Report on Violence and Health, WHO, p. 125)

Concern over the mistreatment of older people has been heightened by the realization that in the coming decades, in both developed and developing countries, there will be a dramatic increase in the population in the older age segment. Old age segment or elders in this context are persons of the age of 60 years and over.

Since the 1970s, a number of cross-cultural exploratory studies all over the world have verified the existence of elder abuse (i.e. Block and Sinnott, 1979; D'Souza, 1971; Desai and Naik 1971; Fujii, 1980; Maldenodo, 1975; Mckain, 1972; Phillips, 1983; Pillemer, 1985; 1987; Quinn and Tomita, 1986; Stoller, 1983; Steinmetz, 1988; Wolf et al. 1984) and have provided some preliminary data on the nature of the problem. Evidence of growing incidence and prevalence is also estimated by increases of Old Age Homes and demand for institutional care and care providers/givers from outside the family (Mala Kapur, Shankardass, 2004). However, the methodological limitations of most of these studies have been such that very little is yet known about the causes and consequences of elder abuse. (Mahajan A. and Madhurima, 1995: 105)

Significance of the Study

Elder abuse is a horrendous problem, growing worse every day as our population ages. Unfortunately the nature and extent of this extremely complex and exacerbating social problem has generally remained hidden from public view. In contrast to its pervasiveness, the problem of abuse of the elderly has received little attention. For that matter we don't even know the number of cases of elder abuse reported annually. Understanding the problem is the key to providing the solution. (Christopher Foote and Christine Stanners, 2002: 49)

Precise knowledge generated through empirical data can form the basis for understanding what constitutes quality of life for elders and for scientific formulations of policy and planning that are data-driven. Someone has rightly suggested that, it may help to form a 'National Elderly Abuse and Neglect Advisory Council' to provide a national perspective on strategies for the care and protection of older people. Also it will be useful to International Network for the Prevention of Elder Abuse, which was formed in 1997, with representation from all six continents.

Interdisciplinary Relevance

Ageing and the matter of abuse and neglect by its very nature is a multi-dimensional problem. It is obvious that it involves perspectives from not only sociology but also family economics / economics, social and behavioral psychology, social work and ethnography / anthropology etc.

Traditional Support System For The Old Aged Persons And Its Gradual Decline:

The problems of senior citizens have been an inherent part of civilization. In the Indian context, the traditional value system was flexible to accommodate the aged. The support system for the person is anchored in the traditional value system and institutional devices. Old age has been a highly respectable stage of life in which not only care is given to the person but he is given power, prestige and privileges in enormous proportion. It is considered a highly important duty of the family members and close relatives to pay utmost respect to the elder members of the family and to seek their blessings. It is also considered an important ideal that the persons should be provided all necessary facilities to fulfil the needs of the persons and to provide them such conducive situation which may provide bliss. There are numbers of sacraments in which the participation of senior citizens is considered to be good. The longer is the age of persons the better protective cover and heavenly bliss are expected to shower over the family. The old age person is considered to be repository of wisdom. With age, the experience of the persons widens. This helps not only to solve the problems of family and kinship networks but also providing the guideline for the performance of religious rituals and customary practices of the family, kinship and caste network. In addition, senior citizens were provided enormous power in the decision making power within the family as also in caste council. The caste panchayat used to be composed of experience persons who used to guide the destiny of the community. Elders ruled both in the family and community affairs. Thus humane values and indispensability of the elders in fulfilling the task of the community provided them a very high place in the society. To neglect the elders and to show disrespect to them was considered to be a great sin and a violation of the normative structure of the society.

The traditional norms, values and behavior patterns were the ideological apparatus which provided a strong defence mechanism not only for the respectable status of the senior citizens but also a mechanism for their survival and welfare. This value system was deeply ingrained among the members of family and community through a continuous and deep process of social learning. Not only the religious scriptures deified old age but the prevalent mores, customs and modes behavior made it obligatory upon the individual to pay respect and to obey them. It was considered a socio-religious duty to follow the advice and dictate of the elders. This helps to prevent problems of social ageing. It created equilibrium in the society which helps to create a balance between the individualistic demands of the younger generations and the sane advices of the older generations. The pervasiveness of the traditional value system help to resolve antagonistic demands of different segments of the society and it was an effective mechanism for conflict resolution.

The traditional value system prevalent in Indian society was actualized through ashramas (the 4 stages of life) and the institutions of family, marriage and kinship organization. Persons belonged to a family which could not dare to disown him. It was a primary duty of a family to provide food, shelter and care to the aged members of the family. Nobody can shun from his /her responsibility to provide adequate care to the aged person. There existed strong primary bond among the members of the family which was also characterized by reciprocity of relationship. Therefore it was a collective responsibility of the family to take care of the old aged persons. In times of distress, illness and disease to the persons the family took the full responsibility for the treatment and rehabilitation of the old aged persons. In such cases the family provided great psychological solace and protection to the persons.

In India the joint Hindu family / extended family has been prevalent norm. In such family male elder/head of the family was considered as the *KARTA* of the family. As head of the family, he controlled the familial assets. This statutory power provided enormous control over the property and related decision making process. Other sharers in the property could not violate the dictates of the elders. The right over the property persisted through the very end of life unless the property is given by elders to the others members of the family through some statutory device. This legal position of the elders in the family was a device to curb the neglect of the elders as others in the family had a fear to be deprived in the share of the family property. Even though the elders may not be having any income of his own and he may also be physically incapable of doing any purposeful activity yet his statutory rights over the family property was a great defence mechanism against his exploitation and mistreatment.

In modern times joint households in India is changing rapidly and has assumed varied forms. Wherever the joint family exists, it is not the male elder but the main bread earner of the family who holds the decision making power. If the main bread earner happens to be a member of the younger generation, his orientation to life and family matters happen to differ considerably from the male elders. This conflict may manifest in form of real or perceived elder neglect or abuse. There are joint families where the earning member is living outside the native place. In such families care of the elder is often being taken over by the female member of the family or by some junior male member. In such situation also the senior citizens may not be taken care by the other family members in satisfactory manner.

The care of the senior citizens also differs considerably in the nuclear cum intermediate family wherein both husband and wife may be earning member of the family and children may be going to school. In such small types family elder male or female may be left behind in the home. They often feel lonely and suffer from loss of close and intimate interaction. The missing human warmth may lead to depression in the elderly.

In modern times the urban and rural family presents different scenario for the care and well being of the elders. Most of the urban families are of small size and have a different life style to maintain occupation and income differentiation among the members of the urban family. The mobility and the fast life style of the members of the family leave little room for the care of the elders. Apart from business families, individual goals may not align with the overall Family and this leaves the non-earning members at a disadvantage.

Apart from family, kinship organization in the traditional society has been other important agency of elder care. The broad network of relatives often helps the elders in times of distress. These relatives may consist of the blood relations or relatives due to marriage alliances. Daughters and sisters even after marriage maintain close relationship with the parental family even after marriage. Whenever father / grandfather are sick and old, these relatives have provided necessary care and support to the elder member of the parental family. Similarly brothers, uncles and close male relatives have also provided care and support to elders. In traditional society, the kinship organization has provided considerable support to the elders.

Another important support system available to elders in the traditional society in India had been the caste system. Not only the elders achieve a place of imminence and power in the caste council but the caste as a whole took care of the elders of the community. With urbanization, gradual erosion of caste panchayat and increasing politicization of the caste, the elders support is not instantly and abundantly available as in the past.

The traditional Indian village was a cohesive and powerful community. Village community served as a vehicle of ordering social relationship and providing cohesiveness. Village was a social unit which created a bond of reciprocal and intimate relationship among the members of the village community. In such community the illness and the death of the elders was considered a sorrowful occasion for the whole community. The village stood behind the elders as a unified whole. With the increasing differentiation and divisions within the village community, it has adversely affected the position of elders in the village community.

In contemporary society support mechanism of the care and welfare of the senior citizens has changed considerably. In the absence of traditional support system the elders feel isolated/ alienated. The structural changes occurring in the contemporary society have made the position of the elders significantly weak. The traditional support mechanism of family, kinship organization and the village community were great helpline to elders. These were reinforced by the social, cultural and religious value system, norms and mode of behavior. All of these are changing rapidly and therefore the status of senior citizens in contemporary society has become somewhat precarious.

In Indian society, as well as, in many developing countries the traditional support systems for elders were the extended family and the kinship network. There was a sense of obligation and reciprocity among the family members who in times of distress used to provide adequate protective care and service to the elders. However, with the rapid socioeconomic changes taking place in contemporary society, the Kith and Kin in the family are gradually withdrawing themselves from such services to elders. The wives, the sons, the brothers used to be the chief care giver to the elders. However, the scenario is changing and changing very fast. Some of the factors which have contributed to the decline of family support are changing nature of joint family, independent earning status of both male and female members. Improving gender role and norms in society have inadvertently created a gap in the household work capacity often with respect to elderly care. There is a demand of 3rd party elder care for familial obligations. But the state institutions are not up to the mark to give satisfactory care.

In urban areas, the alienated elderly often turn to solace of new-age religious groups which also serve as a means of socialization.

The prevailing economic situation has adversely affected the viability of the family. Neither the family based on the earnings of the service sector nor on the self employment sector finds it easy to survive in these hard times. The basic needs of the family are food, schooling of the children and comfortable status in the society anchored in economic self sufficiency. The senior citizens often become victim of economic stringency of the family.

As the longevity of the ageing population has increased, there is much demand on the part of elders for medical and health care, a satisfactory status of the older in the family and a longer period of care giving by the family. This often puts strain on the family resources both in terms of financial support and human support. Thus, there is an erosion of the family support to the elders living within it.

Status of Older Persons and the Problems of Neglect and Abuse

After having discussed the support system available to old aged persons in traditional societies the analysis now proceeds to the status of per sons in modern times. The status and the respect accorded to senior citizens in traditional society's are diminishing in modern times. In traditional societies not only the power and authority of old aged persons were of high orders but in the traditional social network of the family kinship organizations, caste system and village community provided necessary help and care to the old aged persons whenever he was in need of it. With the dwindling of traditional network and the emergence of modern forces of change and transformation, the old aged persons find themselves in a very helpless and precarious situation. Urbanization, industrialization and migration of population from one place to another are making the primary bonds of relationship and the primary institutions increasingly weak. Not only that the new value system based on individualism, advancement of self interest and the desire for upward mobility have made the situation much more adverse. In the highly competitive market economy more and more people are engulfed in rat race for the advancement of power, prestige and monetary gain. The old person in such a situation is being increasingly marginalized. His physical inability and loss of economic power have become more adverse when it is compounded by the self aggrandizement of the family members and immediate kinship network. His utter dependency upon others has reduced his persona as non entity. These precarious situations of the old aged person have multifarious dimensions. It may relate to inadequate supply of food and nourishment, improper care of health or it may extend to isolation, depression and other psychic-dissatisfaction. Sometimes this situation is leading to utter neglect and ostresization of the old aged persons. The result is modern society alternative institutions and socio-legal measures are being to explore to improve the situation of the old aged persons. There are old age home on the one hand and the legal administrative measure on the other hand to protect the interest of the senior citizens. The government machinery and the non-governmental organizations all are working together for the welfare and the protection of the senior citizens.

Thus in modern times not only the support system available to senior citizens are changing from primary institution to secondary institution but it is also a shifting of responsibility reciprocity and intimacy available to senior citizens in the primary institution and groups to the impersonal and indirect relationship which are the hallmark of secondary institutions which are taking charge of the care and welfare of the senior citizens. In the emerging scenario senior citizens not only has the problem of sustenance and survival but also the problem of leading an honourable and dignified life.

Development of Research in the subject

Mistreatment of older people-referred to as "elder abuse"- was first described in British Scientific journals in 1975 under the term "granny battering" (Burston, G.R., 1975; Baker, 1975; Randal J, German T., 1999). In the U.S. these reports were immediately viewed as a socio-political concern, and quickly led to legislative action. In the UK, it took a further 15 years for the issue to receive research and political credence (Ogg and Bennett, 1992: 305: 998-9). The growing world wide focus on the abuse of older people since then has sought to parallel the focus upon human rights, gender equality and especially population ageing (WHO/INPEA, 2002:2).

During the 1980s scientific research and government actions were reported from Australia, Canada, China (Hong Kong SAR), Norway Sweden and the United States, and in the following decade from Argentina, Brazil, Chile, India, Israel, Japan, South Africa, the United Kingdom and other European countries. (World Report on Violence and Health, WHO, P. 125.) Most of the researches on the extent of elder abuse have been inconsistent because of the limited source of data on the problem. However, some of the important studies abroad which have been carried out on elder abuse and neglect are as follows – Mckain (1972), Maldanodo (1975), Block and Sinnott (1979), Briley (1979), Lau and Kosberg (1979), Phillips (1983), Stoller (1983), Wolf et.al. (1984), Pillemer (1985, 1987), Quinn and Tomita (1986), Pillemer and Finkelhor (1988), Pillemer and Suiter (1988) Gelles and Cornell (1990), Galascock and Wagner (1986), O'Malley et.al. (1979), Davidson J.L. (1979), Schiamberg LB, Gans D. (1999), Carp R.M. (2000).

Although elder abuse was first identified in developed countries, where most of the existing research has been conducted, on anecdotal evidence and later reports from some developing countries have shown that it is a universal phenomenon.

In India as early as in 1968, Bose and Gangarade, Sharma (1969), Victor D'Souza (1971) and Desai and Naik (1971) worked on the changing roles and emerging problems of the elderly people. Some other studies (i.e. Nair 1980, Vatik 1980, D'Souza 1982, Bhatia 1983, Desai 1986, Bose 1988, Mahadevan and Smangla 1986, Guha 1992, Sharma 1985, Randhawa and Bhatnagar 1985, Ranade 1984, Prasad, 1984, Mahajan (1987), Mehta (1987), Nagla (1987), Rajeshwar Prasad (1987), Sangwan (1989), Rajan (1989), Sarkar (1989), Sarin (1990), Kumar S. Vijay (1991), Mahadevan et.al. (1992), Dhillon (1992), Dak and Sharma (1987), Sooden (1975), Partha Sarthy (1980), Singh (1970), Bali (1995), Punia et.al. (1987), Joshi (2006) etc.) are also there wherein the researchers have highlighted the changing status and living arrangements of the elderly people. The Ministry of Welfare, Govt. of India had also sponsored studies on problems of the aged in 1990. The studies have been completed by several scholars (like Khan, Muthayya and Aneesuddin, Hussain, Shah and Joshi, Upadhyay, Gurumurthy, Nayar and Shanthakumari, Mukherjee, Mishra, Dandekar, Sinha, Sati, Raja, Ahmed and Srivastava, A.R.N.). Kohli (1996) has compiled the findings of these studies.

Scientific analysis of elder abuse- the context, the nature, the process and the outcome-has not been made on scale in India to enable application to comparative macro level situation. (Nayar, P.K.B., 2004: 6)

In India, sociological studies on elder abuse in the family are rare (for example Mahajan and Madhurima (1995), Bhatt, VN. (2004), Krupalani, HS (2004) Rathi Devi (2006) etc.). However, few important studies are there in psychology and other discipline (Ramamurti and Jamuna, 1999; Jamuna and Padmasree, 2000; Prakash, 1998 etc.). Few years back Centre for Gerontological Studies, Thiruvananthapuram organised a national seminar (2004) on 'Abuse, Neglect and Violence of the Elderly', wherein several sociologists have presented their paper. We may mention their names as P.K.B. Nayar, A. Ramanamma, D. Sundaram, A. Bhoite, J.J. Kattakayam, V.N. Bhat, M.T. Bendre, S. Bhattachariya, B. Nalini, J.N. Merlin, M. Purvachar, Mala Kapur Shankardass Arvind K. Joshi etc. Despite of this we find that papers based on empirical observations on the elder abuse in India are really few. For a better understanding of the phenomena, we need knowledge on nature and extent of elder abuse. In other words, there is a need of in depth empirical studies across regions and cultures.

The phenomena of elder abuse in Indian setting has been viewed and analysed in dependency framework (Mahajan and Madhurima: 1995) It is worth mentioning here, that to accommodate the complexity of elder abuse and the many factors associated with it, researchers have turned to the ecological model which was first applied to the study of child abuse and neglect (Garbarino J, Crouter A. (1978)) and has been applied more recently to elder abuse (Schiamberg LB, Gans D. (1999), Carp RM (2000)). The ecological model consists of a nested hierarchy of four levels of the environment: individual, relationship, community and society. The same model will be applied in this research work too.

Objectives: The objectives of the study were –

1. To know the socio-economic background and living conditions of the aged.
2. To know the various problems of the aged.
3. To identify the type of abuse directed towards the elders.
4. To figure out the trends (increasing or decreasing) in elder abuse.
5. To identify and prioritize the factors / causes (individual, relationship, community and society) responsible for abuse.

6. To identify the chief abuser.
7. To suggest measures to prevent elder abuse in the family/community.

Methodology

The design of research is exploratory.

Studies on elder abuse have tended to focus on interpersonal and family problems. Keeping in mind the limitations of earlier studies, an integrated ecological model encompassing individual, interpersonal, community and societal perspectives has been applied.

Research Questions

1. What are the socio-economic background and living conditions of senior citizens ?
2. What are the various problems of senior citizens ?
3. What type of abuse is generally prevalent ?
4. What are the factors of abuse ?
5. Who is the main abuser ?
6. What can be done to stop elder abuse ?

Universe and Sampling

The universe of the present study consists of all the elderly people of Varanasi District who have attained the age of 60 years or above.

On the basis of purposive random sampling we have selected 505 respondents from 16 villages, 2 villages from each blocks of Varanasi namely Kashi Vidyapeeth, Arajiline, Sevapuri, Baragaon, Pindra, Cholapur, Harahua and Chiraigaon. We have also selected 505 urban respondents from all the five zones of Nagar Nigam namely Aadampur, Bhelupura, Varuna Paar, Dashaswamedh and Kotwali. While selecting the sample it was kept in mind to include the aged of various categories and areas. Further, in selecting households and respondents the incidental-cum-purposive sampling technique was adopted. Only those elderly persons willing to make themselves available for interview have been included in the Sample. 5 rural respondents were found unwilling to make themselves avåilable for interview have been excluded from the sample.

Household/family was the basic unit of the sampling. However, the elderly person was the key respondent to the interview-schedule.

Thus, 1005 respondents both from rural (500) and urban (505) areas formed the sample for the present study.

Data Collection: Key Instruments

For the purpose of empirical data collection interview-schedule was the key instrument. An interview-schedule in vernacular language i.e. Hindi (See appendix B). Both open-ended and closed questions were there in accordance with the objectives of the study. It was pre-tested on 5 elderly respondents, both men and women and on the basis of their inputs it was revised and finalized. The interview-schedules were administered individually through personal interview method.

Another technique used in this research was Focus Group discussions (FGDs). The purpose of the FGDs was to know how the senior citizens defined abuse and neglect and also their perception of abuse and neglect. Also with this we tried to identify abused elderly.

Focus Group discussions were conducted on different dates at different places. All FGDs were conducted in the morning as it was found easier and convenient too, to contact elderly persons during morning walk time. The FGDs in the urban area were conducted at following places: (i) Near Vishwanath Temple, BHU (ii) Beniabag park (iii) Shahid Udyaan, Sigra (iv) Durgakund Park (v) Kedar ghat (vi) Near DLW Stadium, and at (vii) Sarnath Park. However, in rural area it was found quite difficult to conduct FGDs the way it was done easily in the urban Varanasi, because of the disturbances created by the local crowd who assembled there very often due to curiosity. We conducted FGDs in rural setting at only three places: (i) Karoundhi (ii) Takkhu ki Bowli, Sewapuri, and (iii) Chiraigaon.

Area of the Study

The study has been conducted at Varanasi, both in selected urban and rural segments. Varanasi is perhaps the only city in the world which is known by three names popularly Kashi, Varanasi and Banaras. As far as the continuity of a classical cultural tradition is concerned it even surpasses all the civilization of the world and holds a unique position. It is very often called the cultural capital of India, where one can see the glimpses of Indian culture.

Varanasi is located in the Gangetic Plain of Uttar Pradesh. It had a population of 3,138,670 in 2011. Out of the total Varanasi population for 2011 census, 43.43 percent lives in urban regions of district. In total 1599260 people lives in urban areas of which males are 847348 and females are 751912. Sex ratio in urban region in 887 as per 2011 census data. 56.57 percent population of Varanasi district lives in rural areas (total 2082934, male = 1081293 and females =1001641). In the rural area sex ratio 926 females per 1000 males.

Some other important information in brief is as below:

Geographical Area (2011)	= 1535 sq. km.
No. of Tehsil	= 2
No. of Block	= 8
No. of Nyay Panchayat	= 108
No. of Gram Panchyat	= 702
No. of Villages	= 1327
(i) Inhabited	= 1289
(ii) Uninhabited	= 38
Town / Group of Towns (2001)	= 4
(i) Nagar Nigam	= 1
(ii) Nagar Palika Parishad	= 1
(iii) Nagar Panchyat	= 1
(iv) Cantonment Board	= 1
Sex Ratio	= 909
Density	= 2399 per sq. km.
Literacy	= 77.05 per cent
(i) Male	= 85.12 per cent
(ii) Female	= 68.20 per cent

Varanasi is a traditional city were cultural change hurts the aged.

Case Studies

For in-depth study a bunch case studies (total 13) has been done to bring out the factors/causes of abuse/abuser. Further, while selecting elderly for case study, special care has been taken to have their representation from all segments of elderly population.

Besides this, we have also done several informal interviews with the elderly and other knowledgeable persons and also with caregivers just to understand the hidden dimensions of the problem.

Operational Definitions

Elder abuse

In public and academic discourses in India their is no consensus about the exact definition of 'elder abuse' (Shankardass, Mala Kapur, 2010: 191).

For the purpose of the present study, we have adopted the definition of abuse from the Action on Elder Abuse (UK), "*abuse is a single or repeated act or lack of appropriate action occurring in any relationship where there is an expectation of trust, which causes harm or distress to an older person.*"

Further, under abuse we have included several categories of abuse such as **physical abuse** (use of any type of physical force), **verbal abuse** (verbal assaults), **socio-psychological abuse** (threat, insult, humiliation, harassment, social isolation etc.) **financial abuse** (grabing money or property and/or any illegal or improper use of elderly persons money or property) and **neglect** (refusal or failure to fulfill any essential requirements like food, clothing, shelter, medicine, treatment etc, obligations or care toward an older person). We have mentioned different forms of abuse in the concerned chapter.

Senior Citizens

Any individual male or female who has attained the age of 60 years or above.

Elderly respondent

An elderly respondent is defined as an individual male or female, who has attained the age of 60 years or more than that at the time of the study, living with the family in the study area.

Nuclear family

A married couple living with unmarried children.

Intermediate family

A married couple living with unmarried children and one of the parent of husband or wife.

Joint family

Two or more generations of members where at least two married couples should be there (for example parents with married son and their unmarried children) living under one roof and sharing food from a common kitchen.

Extended Family

Two or more generations of members where at least more then two married couples should be there (for example parents with married son's and their unmarried children) with other adult or minor members living under one roof and sharing food from a common kitchen.

Data Collection

Primary data collection was done mostly by Principal Investigator and some time by project fellow too.

After completing the data collection in rural and urban areas of Varanasi, final coding was done to convert qualitative data into quantitative data. Licenced SPSS was not available with us, therefore, we have done classification and tabulation manually. We have not used inferential statistical tests, only simple and cross tables were prepared. We have examine the relationship between different variables under study. Cased studies were done to understand the whole issue easily.

Chapter - 3

Socio- Economic Background

In this chapter the socio-economic background of the respondents has been presented. For any analysis of the elderly population it is important to know their socio-economic characteristics like age, literacy, gender, marital status, work participation rate, etc. All these socio-economic characteristics are highly correlated with longevity, living standards and quality of life (Granahan, 1992; Rajan et al, 1999; Mayers 1986; Rajan, 1989, 1982; Kumar, 1991; Sharma and Dak 1987; Nandal et al 1987; Singh et al; 1987; Dandekar, 1996, Joshi, 2006 etc.).

Age and Residential Background

The distribution of respondents on the basis of age and residential background are presented in the table number 3.1

Table 3.1: Distribution of respondents according to age

Age (in years)	*Urban*	*Rural*	*Total*
60-69	285 (56.4)	195 (39.0)	480 (48.2)
70-79	170 (33.7)	210 (42.0)	380 (38.2)
80+	50 (9.9)	95 (19.0)	145 (13.6)
Total	**505 (50.2)**	**500 (49.8)**	**1005 (100.0)**

Note: Figures in the brackets are percentage.

From the above table it is obvious that 48.2 percent respondents are of the age between 60 to 69 years (young –old), 38.2 percent are between 70 to 79 years (old-old) and remaining 13.6 percent are 80 years or more in age (oldest-old). To conclude we can say that majority of the respondents are of 'young old' category i.e. between

60 to 69 years of age. Further, when we compare on the basis of rural-urban background and the distribution of respondents according to age, we found that young-old are more in urban areas while old-old are more in rural areas.

Gender

Studies by Kivela et al, 1992; Wolf, 1997; NCEA, 1998 & 2006, Srinivas, 2004; and Chokkanathan and Lee, 2005; Devi Prasad, 2008 etc. have found that the majority of elderly victims are women. Therefore, it is important here to analyze gender-wise distribution of our respondents. The gender-wise distribution of our respondents is presented in the following table.

Table 3.2: Distribution of respondents according to gender

Gender	*Frequency*	*Percentage*
Male	842	83.8
Female	163	16.2
Total	**1005**	**100.0**

It is obvious from the above table that 83.8 percent respondents are male and only 16.2 percent are females. We can say that majority of the elderly respondents are male. It is worth mentioning here that feminization of ageing is taking place in India. Since for primary data collection the male senior citizens were available easily, therefore,in this study males are in majority.

Age and sex-wise distribution of respondents clearly shows that majority (53.2 %) of the male respondents are in young-old category, while females (55.2%) are in old-old category (Table 3.3 and Fig. 3.1).

Table 3.3: Age and Sex- wise distribution of respondents

Age / Sex	*Male*	*Female*	*Percentage*
60-69 years	448 (53.2)	32 (19.6)	480 (48.2)
70-79 years	290 (34.4)	90 (55.2)	380 (38.2)
80+ years	104 (12.4)	41 (25.2)	145 (13.6)
Total	**842 (83.8)**	**163 (16.2)**	**1005 (100.0)**

Note: Bracket indicates percentage

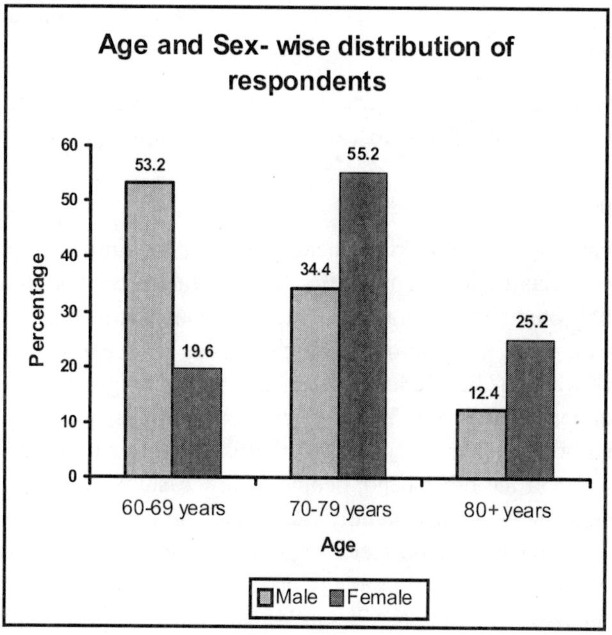

Fig. 3.1

Religion

We have also collected information about the religion of our respondents. Religion -wise distribution of respondents is presented as below.

Table 3.4: Distribution of respondents according to religion

Religion	*Frequency*	*Percentage*
Hindu	903	89.8
Islam	87	8.7
Sikh	15	1.5
Total	**1005**	**100.0**

It is obvious from the above table that 89.8 percent respondents were Hindus, 8.7 percent were Muslims and remaining 1.5 percent was Sikh. To conclude, we can say that majority of the respondents were Hindus. It is significant that the proportion of Muslim respondents is comparatively small in relation with their share in the general population

Further, this is for information that only one Christian lady was there in our sample but before we get her interviewed she died.

Caste

Caste in India is an important social institution that influences almost every aspects of individual's life. In rural India, caste system still dominates the socio-cultural life- the functions, status, opportunities etc. of the villagers. Traditionally higher castes have several privileges while lower caste people suffered certain civil and religious disabilities. The upper caste people have larger land holdings, joint families, comparatively better education and a different culture of thinking and behavior. On the other hand, people of low caste posses low socio-economic status, nuclear family; sometimes broken family also, and several handicaps and obstacles to greater vertical mobility. Many of the poor aged persons continue to do hard labour-intensive work for their survival (Joshi, A.K., 2006: 74). In view of this we have also tried to know the caste of Hindu respondents (N=903). Caste–wise distribution of Hindu respondents is as below.

Table 3.5: Distribution of respondents according to caste

N=903

Caste Category	*Frequency*	*Percentage*
General or Upper Caste	301	33.3
Backward Caste	407	45.1
Scheduled Caste	180	9.9
Scheduled Tribes	15	1.7
Total	**903**	**100.0**

It is obvious from above table that 33.3 percent respondents belong to general *(Savarna)* or upper caste, 45.1 percent respondents belong to backward castes, 20.0 percent respondents belong to scheduled caste and remaining only 1.7 percent belongs to scheduled tribes. They reported their religion as Hindu. To conclude, we may say that majority of the respondents belong to backward castes which is roughly in proportion to their share in the general population (Table 3.5 and Fig. 3.2).

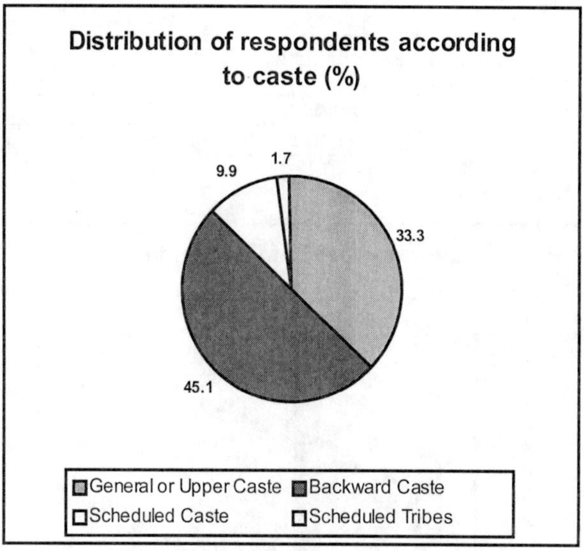

Fig. 3.2

Literacy Level

It is obvious from the following table that the educational level of majority of respondents (25.9 %) is up to High School. Further, 14.7 percent respondents are illiterate while 17.9 percent respondents are only literate i.e. they can only make signature of their own.11.5 percent respondents possess post graduate qualifications or even more (2.6%).13.1 percent respondents are educated up to graduate level. More women (23.3%) were found to be illiterate as against men (13.1%) (Table 3.6 and Fig. 3.3). Further enquiry regarding their professional and technical qualifications revealed that 2 percent of them possess professional and technical qualifications too, like B. Ed, M. Ed, LL.B, M.B.B.S, M.D., C.A., I.T.I or Polytechnic diploma etc.

Table 3.6: Literacy level of Respondents

Educational Level	*Male*	*Female*	*Percentage*
Illiterate	110 (13.1)	38 (23.3)	148 (14.7)
Only Literate	160 (19.0)	20 (12.3)	180 (17.9)
Up to High School	200 (23.7)	60 (36.8)	260 (25.9)

(*Contd...*)

Intermediate	128 (15.2)	15 (9.2)	143 (14.3)
Graduate	118 (14.0)	14 (8.6)	132 (13.1)
Post Graduate	105 (12.5)	11 (6.7)	116 (11.5)
Doctorate	21 (2.5)	5 (3.1)	26 (2.6)
Total	**842 (83.8)**	**163 (16.2)**	**1005 (100.0)**

Note: Bracket indicates percentage.

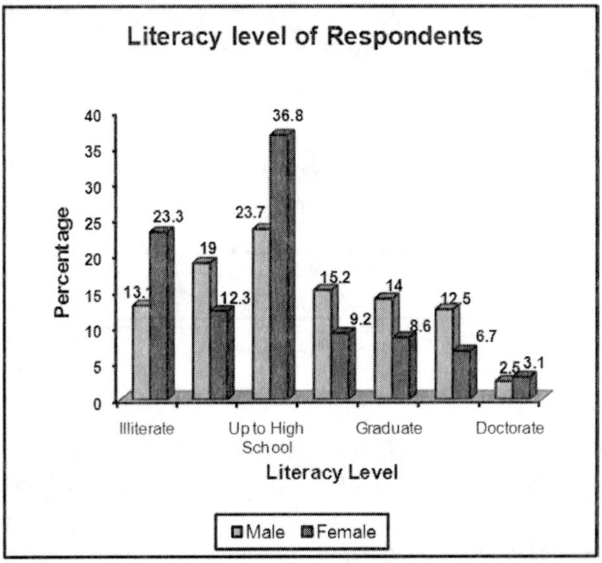

Fig. 3.3

Marital Status

During old age marital status plays an important role as it has important implications for the care and support of elderly. According to V.N. Bhat (2006:133), marital status has the greatest impact on living arrangements of the elderly population. Easwaramoorthy's study (1991) also confirms this. Marital status of the elderly influences the social status and the social relationships of the elderly men and women. Keeping in view of this we have tried to know marital status of our respondents, which is presented in the following table.

It is obvious from the above table that majority of the respondents (72.3 %) are married. 27 percent of respondents are widowed and 0.4 percent is separated. Further, we have found that 0.3 percent of the respondents are unmarried. All of them are female and from urban area. When we compare marital status of male and female we find that more men (80.4%) are in the married category and more women (65.0%) among the widowed category. Widowed status brings a very tough time during old age for both male and female elderly. A widow has to face all the problems of biological aging with all sorts of discriminations and emotional disruption. Widowhood has important consequences for the dependency ratio of the elderly especially of the female elderly.

Table 3.7: Marital Status Wise Distribution of Respondents

Marital Status	*Male*	*Female*	*Percentage*
Married	677 (80.0)	50 (30.7)	727 (72.3)
Unmarried	0 (0.0)	3 (1.8)	3 (0.3)
Widowed	165 (19.6)	106 (65.0)	271 (27.0)
Separated	0 (0.0)	4 (2.5)	4 (0.4)
Total	**842 (83.8)**	**163 (16.2)**	**1005 (100.0)**

Note: Bracket indicates percentage

Duration of Stay

We have also collected information regarding respondent's duration of stay at Varanasi. We have found that majority (66.7%) of the respondents were living in Varanasi since birth. 7.7 percent were found living since less than last ten years, 9.9 percent were living in Varanasi since last 11 to 20 years, 5.8 percent were living in Varanasi since last 21 to 30 years and remaining 9.9 percent were living since last 30 years or more. (See table below)

Table 3.8: Distribution of respondents according to their stay in Varanasi

Duration	*Urban*	*Rural*	*Total*
Since birth	210 (41.6)	460 (92.0)	670 (66.7)
Less than 10 years	67 (13.3)	10 (2.0)	77 (7.7)
11-20 years	80 (15.8)	20 (4.0)	100 (9.9)
21-30 years	48 (9.5)	10 (2.0)	58 (5.8)
31+ years	100 (19.8)	-	100 (9.9)
Total	**505 (50.2)**	**500 (49.8)**	**1005 (100.0)**

Note: Bracket indicates percentage

8 percent of the respondents though normally living in rural areas are actually residing in new housing colonies that have come up on the

urban fringes. The anomaly has arisen because the limits of Nagar-Nigam Varanasi have not been extended since last three decades or more. Otherwise, these colonies are populated by people with service in professional occupations and they have all urban facilities. In this study they have been included in rural segment.

Nature of Family

The structure and functions of family are changing due to several socio-economic reasons. Several studies are there which have proved that traditional joint families are disintegrating and converting into nuclear families. In India an elderly person gets support and care from the family. Therefore, it is essential to know nature of the family of our respondents.

Table 3.9: Distribution of respondents according to types of family

Family types	*Men*	*Women*	*Total*
Nuclear	199 (23.6)	21 (12.9)	220 (21.8)
Intermediate	277 (32.9)	84 (51.5)	361 (36.0)
Joint	292 (34.7)	42 (25.8)	334 (33.2)
Extended	74 (8.8)	16 (9.8)	90 (9.0)
Total	**842 (83.8)**	**163 (16.2)**	**1005 (100.0)**

It is obvious from above table that majority (36.0%) of the respondent's family is intermediate. 33.2 percent respondent's family is joint, 21.8 per cent's nuclear and 9.0 percent respondent's family is extended. To conclude, we may say that majority of the respondents' families are intermediate in nature.

Table 3.10: Distribution of respondents according to their family size

Family Members	*Men*	*Women*	*Total*
Two only	195 (23.2)	16 (9.8)	211 (21.0)
3 to 6 members	180 (21.4)	71 (43.6)	251 (24.9)
7 to 9 members	406 (48.2)	64 (39.3)	470 (46.8)
10+	61 (7.2)	12 (7.3)	73 (7.3)
Total	**842 (83.8)**	**163 (16.2)**	**1005 (100.0)**

With regard to size of the family it was found that in the majority of the cases it's 7 to 9 members. In the case of 24.9 percent respondents the family size is 3 to 6 members, while in 7.3 percent family size is

10 or more members. The remaining 21 percent respondents' families have 2 members only.

Living Arrangements

Living arrangement is an important variable to understand the status of the aged persons. It determines the quality of life of elderly in many ways. Generally in India, an elderly person or the parents love to live with their elder son's family. However, several other forms of living arrangements are also found.

Table 3.11: Living arrangements of the respondent

S.No.	*Arrangements*	*Frequency*	*Percentage*
1.	Living with wife/husband	211	21.0
2.	Living with brother's family	17	1.7
3.	Living with Son/Son's family	357	35.5
4.	Living with daughter/daughter's family	3	0.3
5.	Living with spouse, children and grand children	410	40.8
6.	Living with sister	2	0.2
7.	Living with daughter-in-law and grand children	5	0.5
	Total	**1005**	**100.0**

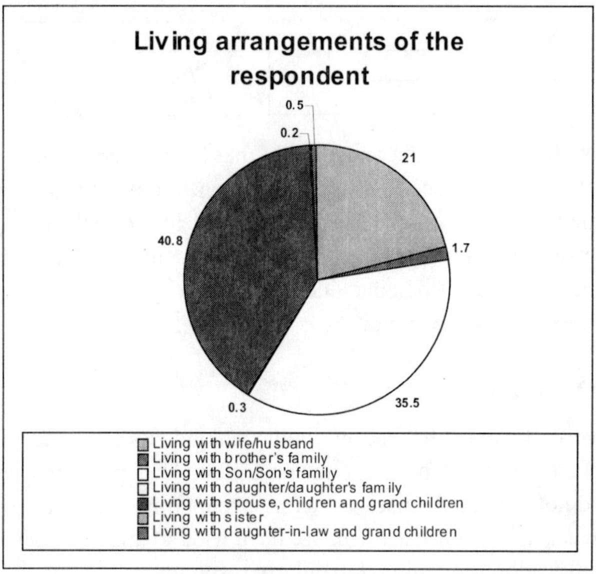

Fig. 3.4

It is obvious from the above table that more than one third (35.5%) of the respondents are living with son/son's family, 21.0 percent are living with their spouse, 1.7 percent with brother's family, 0.3 percent with daughter's family. The largest number, i.e. 40.8 percent with spouse, children and grand children, 0.2 percent with sister and remaining 0.5 percent with daughter-in-law and grand children. To conclude, if we add the two over lapping arranges 3 and 5, evidently the common form of living arrangement reported was living with son/son's family (Table 3.11 and Fig. 3.4).

Ownership of House

One of the important determinants of the well being of an individual is housing. Before coming to analyse living space within the house, it is better to know first, about the ownership of house.

Table 3.12: Distribution of respondents according to ownership of their residence

Ownership of Residential House	*Frequency*	*Percentage*
Self/Spouse	830	82.6
Son's	125	12.4
Brother's	5	0.5
Daughter/Daughter-in-laws	3	0.3
Rented house	42	4.2
Total	**1005**	**100.0**

It is obvious from the above table that 82.6 percent respondents live in their own house, 12.4 percent live with their son, 0.5 percent live in their brother's house, 0.3 percent respondent stay in their daughter/daughter-in-law's house and remaining 4.2 percent respondents live in rented houses. It may be concluded that majority of the respondents (87.6%) live in their own houses.

Main Occupation

We have collected information about respondents past and current occupation. It is worth mentioning that 65 female respondents has said they had not engage themselves to any occupation, they were simply housewives after their marriage. We have tried to analyze occupation wise distribution remaining 940 elderly respondents.

Table below shows the main occupation of the respondents when they were not old.

Table 3.13: Distribution of respondents according to their main occupation

N=940

Occupation	*Frequency*	*Percent*
Service	320	34.0
Business	80	8.5
Agriculture/Farming	310	33.0
Agricultural labour	105	11.2
Self employed	20	2.1
Animal husbandry/dairying	31	3.3
Unskilled work	74	7.9
Total	**940**	**100.00**

It is obvious from the above table that the main occupation of the 34.0 percent respondents was service while 8.5 percent respondents' main occupation was business, 33.0 percent respondents were agricultural labour, 2.1 percent were self employed as doctor (medico), contractor etc., 3.3 percent were doing cattle rearing work, remaining 7.9 percent respondents occupation was unskilled work like rickshaw-puller, labourer, trolley puller or other unskilled work. It may be concluded that majority of the respondents' occupation was service and related to agricultural work.

The vast majority of India's labour force of nearly four hundred eighty million is employed in the informal sector, which is characterized by insecurity of employment, poor working conditions, very low or zero saving capacity and absence of social security. This is where the self-employed, such as small farmers and entrepreneurs, artisans, street vendors and rickshaw pullers, are clubbed together with wage workers in farms, unorganized enterprises and households (Common Cause, 2012:1). The formal organized sector, includes the state and its instrumentalities, the corporate and large not-for-profit organizations. In India about 11 percent working population is in formal or organised sector, remaining 89 percent people work in the unorganized sector. We have also tried to find from our service class respondents about the sector in which they were employed. The information received is presented in the table below.

Table 3.14: Distribution of respondents according to sector wise service

N= 320

Service Sector	*Frequency*	*Percent*
Formal/Organized	128	40.0
Informal/Unorganized	192	60.0
Total	**320**	**100.0**

It is obvious from above table that 40 percent of respondents have worked in the formal sector wherein majority (60.0%) of the respondents had worked in informal sector. By this information we may draw an inference about the financial status/ security of the elderly. Indeed, actually speaking the term 'retirement' scarcely applies to people retiring from informal/unorganized sector employment. They hardly get any financial benefit. They are simply discarded after they are considered too old to do their job. They are the most vulnerable to neglect and abuse. In comparison the formal sector employees get pensionary and other benefit on their retirement.

Period of Superannuation

We have also tried to know from our 320 respondents about when they retired from service. It was found that 36.1 percent of them retired within last 10 years, 45.4 percent retired within last 11 to 20 years and the remaining 18.5 percent retired more than 21 years ago. To conclude we can say that majority of the respondents superannuated 11 to 20 years ago. (See table below)

Table 3.15: Distribution of respondents according to retirement period

N=320

Retirement period	*Frequency*	*Percent*
Within 10 years	119	36.1
11-20 years	150	45.4
21+	61	18.5
Total	**330**	**100.0**

Current Working Status

As regard current working status, the details are presented in the following table.

Table 3.16: Distribution of respondents according to their current working status

Current working status	*Frequency*	*Percent*
Working	636	63.3
Not working	369	36.7
Total	**1005**	**100.0**

It is obvious from the above table that 63.3 percent of our respondents are still working while 36.7 percent of them are not working. To conclude we may say that still despite of so much of age 63.3.percent of respondents are still working. Majority (62.8%) of the working elderly are from rural areas. In urban areas elderly businessmen, professionals and vendors/shop keepers are found working. Also, a few poor urban elderly were also found doing unskilled work.

Current Occupation

636 respondents are still working. Their current occupation is presented in the following table.

Table 3.17: Distribution of respondents according to their current occupation

N=636

Current Occupation	*Frequency*	*Percent*
Unskilled work	196	30.8
Caste based occupations	36	5.7
Business	14	2.2
Cultivation	310	48.7
Self employed	16	2.5
Petty Business/Vender	64	10.1
Total	**636**	**100.0**

It is obvious from the above table that majority of respondents (48.7%) are still doing agricultural work. 30.8 percent of the respondents are doing unskilled work, 10.1 percent petty business or working as a vendor, 5.7 percent caste based occupation, 2.5 percent self-employed and remaining 2.2 percent are doing business.

To conclude, we may say that majority of them are doing labour intensive work despite of their old age. In fact the term 'retirement' applies to the employed persons only, and to the self employed, nor to the informal sector labourers, toilers and peasants.

Income of the respondent

As regards to monthly income of respondents, we find that 19.4 percent respondents have no income at all, followed by around 48 percent having an income upto Rs. 5000/- per month. 13.9 percent respondents' income is between Rs. 5001 to 10,000/-, 10.5 percent respondents income is between 10001 to 15000/-, 5 percent respondents income is 15001 Rs. to 20000 and remaining 3.4 percent respondents income is 20001 or more. The respondents whose income is more than 15000/- per month are mostly from urban areas and that too they are Pensioners.

Sex-wise distribution of monthly income status clearly shows that majority (52.1 percent) of the female respondents have no income at all (See table 3.18 and Fig. 3.5).

Table 3.18: Distribution of respondents according to their monthly income (from all sources)

Monthly family income (in Rs.)	*Male*	*Female*	*Total*
No Income	110 (13.1)	85 (52.1)	195 (19.4)
Less than 5000	421 (50.0)	59 (36.2)	480 (47.8)
5001 to 10000	135 (16.0)	5 (3.1)	140 (13.9)
10001 to 15000	98 (11.6)	8 (4.9)	106 (10.5)
15001 to 20000	46 (5.5)	4 (2.5)	50 (5.0)
20,001+	32 (3.8)	2 (1.2)	34 (3.4)
Total	**842 (83.8)**	**163 (16.2)**	**1005 (100.0)**

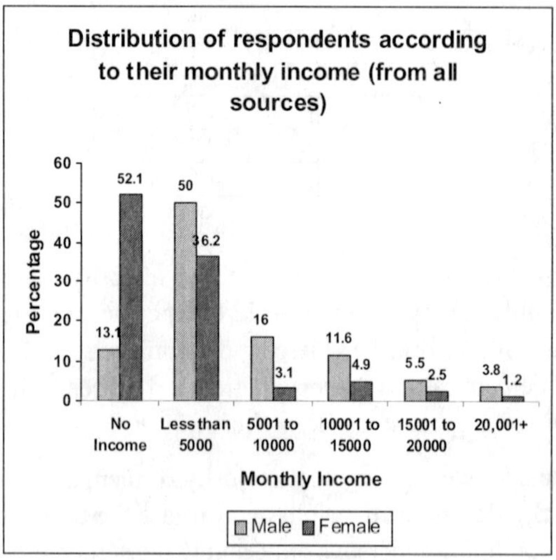

Fig. 3.5

Living separately from family members

As regards separation from family members, it is obvious from the table below that majority (53.9%) of respondents said that their family members are living separately from them.

Table 3.19: Distribution of respondents according to separately living family members

Living separately	*Frequency*	*Percent*
Yes	542	53.9
No	463	46.1
Total	1005	100.0

From the above data we may conclude that majority of the respondents family members are living separately.

We have also tried to know the reasons of their family members living separately and the reasons given are presented in the following table.

Table No. 3.20: Reasons for living separately

N=542*

Reasons	*Per cent*
Selfishness	64.2
Family Tension	35.8
Due to exigency of service/business	69.0
Shortage of living space in the house	28.0
Got property from in-laws or relatives	18.5
Don't like locality	12.7

* Total of percentage is more than 100 as some of the respondents have given more than one reasons.

It is obvious from the above table that the majority of respondents (69.0%) family members are living separately due to demands of service or business, while 64.2 percent are living separately due to sheer selfishness. 35.8 percent of the respondent's family members are not living together due to some short of family tension. However there are some other reasons too, for living separately. For example, 28 percent of the respondent's family members are living separately due to shortage of space, 18.5 percent members are living separately as they have received gift of land or house from their near and dear relative and 12.7 percent respondents family members are not living together as they don't like that particular locality.

Hence we may say that there are several reasons for living separately. Also these reasons vary from member to member of the same family.

Problems of Senior Citizens

Senior Citizens have to face various types of problems. Broadly we may put these problems into three main categories: health, economic and socio-psychological. Since older persons are not a homogeneous group, we have tried to know from our respondents that what are the major problems of old age. The findings are presented in the table below.

Table 3.21: Distribution of respondents according to perception of major problems of old age*

Major problems	*Percentage*
Health and medical problems	98.2
Socio-psychological problem	77.8
Economic problems	89.5

* Multiple responses

It is obvious from the above table that majority (98.2%) of our respondents have mentioned health and medical problems as the major problem of senior citizens. 89.5 percent of them have mentioned economic problems and 77.8 percent of them socio-psychological problems major problems old age.

Chapter - 4

Family Life and Socio-Psychological Interactions

In this chapter we have revealed the facts about respondents' role in the decision making process, fulfillment of their needs by family members, possession of a separate room in the house by them, room occupancy at the time of guest's arrival, having freedom to visit guests, their feelings during arrival of guest, their main care givers, freedom to mix with their grand children, altercation with family members, satisfaction with the facilities provided by the family members, friend's visits, their visits to friends, nature of hospitality to their friends by the family member, relationship with neighbours, family members taking/or accompanying them to tourist/ religious places, changing attitude of family and its reasons, incidence of their participation in domestic work, availability of a servant to take care of them, feeling of neglect, unhappiness with family members and its reasons etc.

Participation in the decision making process

Participation in the decision making process of family is an important indicator of status of an elderly person. Keeping this in view we have enquired from our respondents the areas/issues on which their advice is sought by their family members.

Table 4.1: Distribution of respondents according to the areas on which advice is sought

N= 1005*

Matters on which elders advice sought	*Frequency*	*Percentage*
Marriage related	880	87.6
Family affairs	590	58.7
Children's education	345	34.3
Property related matters	620	61.7
Occupation related matters	370	36.8
Health related matters	460	45.8
Business/farming related matters	642	63.9
Any matter sometimes	280	27.9
No advice taken	125	12.4
Advice on all important matters	800	79.6

* Multiple responses

It is obvious from the above table that participation of our respondents in the decision-making process on family affairs is satisfactory. It is found that majority of the respondents give advice on almost all the important matters especially marriage related matters, business, or farming related matters and matters relating to property. It is no less important to know that 12.4 percent respondents are also there whose advice is not taken on any matter. We have tried to explore reasons behind this. It was found that it was because they did not get any importance from their family.

Availability of Food

Some aspects of ageing can be postponed up to some extent, if elderly persons maintain their health by nutritious food, regular exercise and good health practice. But several elderly persons find it difficult to get nutritious food due to poverty or due to negligence of care givers.

In this context we have tried to find out from our respondents about availability of nutritious food to them. The responses are presented in the table below –

Table 4.2: Distribution of respondents according to availability of nutritious food

Availability	*Frequency*	*Percent*
Yes	337	33.5
No	668	66.5
Total	**1005**	**100.0**

It is clear from the above table No.4.2 that 33.5 percent respondents have said that they get nutritious food, while majority of them (66.5%) has said that they don't get it.

To conclude, majority of the elderly people don't get nutritious food, not even milk and seasonal fruits. (See table no.4.3 below).

Table 4.3: Distribution of respondents according to availability of milk and seasonal fruits

Availability	*Frequency*	*Percent*
Yes	281	28.0
No	724	72.0
Total	**1005**	**100.0**

Need fulfillment

We have also tried to know from our respondents if their on liner needs are fully met by their children. The responses are presented in the following table.

Table 4.4: Distribution of respondent according to fulfillment of their needs by children

N=980

Satisfaction of Needs	*Frequency*	*Percentage*
Yes	720	73.5
No	260	26.5
Total	**980**	**100.0**

A large majority (73.5 %) of the respondents have said that their needs are fulfilled by their children. On the other side, about one-fourths of respondents (26.5 %) have disclosed that their needs are not fulfilled by their children. To conclude, we may say that the needs of significant numbers of respondents are not fulfilled.

Respect from family members

We have tried to know from our respondents about getting proper respect from their family members. The responses are presented in the following table.

Table 4.5: Distribution of respondents according to getting adequate respect from family member

Degree of Respect	*Frequency*	*Percentage*
Adequate	777	77.3
Not adequate	228	22.7
Total	**1005**	**100.0**

It is obvious from the above table that 77.3 percent of our respondents are of the opinion that they are getting proper respect from their family members. Still, there are 22.7 percent of respondents, who feel that they are not getting proper respect from them.

To conclude, we may say that elderly persons are not getting the amount of respect as they were given in earlier days. When we further tried to probe we found that 38.6 percent respondents feel that a filial respect is declining due to their old age. (See table below)

Table 4.6: Distribution of respondents according to their views on declining respect due to old age

Views	*Frequency*	*Percentage*
Yes	617	61.4
No	388	38.6
Total	**1005**	**100.0**

Provision of Separate Room

For privacy and comfort, a separate room is required for the elderly person. Generally due to paucity of space or in many cases due to neglect or ignorance, family members don't provide a separate room to the elderly member. In rural areas, this type of provision is very rare and even, in the rich families generally. They get living space in the outer part of the house. The responses received on this aspect are presented in the following table.

Table 4.7: Distribution of respondents according to provision of separate room in the house

Provision of separate room	*Frequency*	*Percentage*
Yes	307	30.5
No	698	69.5
Total	**1005**	**100.0**

It is obvious from the above table that only 30.5 percent respondents have the facility of a separate room in the houses, while the majority (69.5%) of them doesn't have such facility. When we tried to probe further, we found that majority of the upper or middle class, particularly those owing houses urban respondents have a separate room to themselves. The rural respondents generally don't possess rooms; they stay during night in the outer part, of the main house on a separate section usually called 'baithaka' which is also shared by a guest or visitor.

Table 4.8: Distribution of respondents according to room occupancy at the time of guests' arrival

N=307

Response	*Frequency*	*Percentage*
Have to vacate	40	13.0
Don't have to vacate	267	87.0
Total	**307**	**100.0**

It is obvious from the above table that at least 13 percent respondents have to vacate their room on a guest's arrival. To vacate their room might create several problems to the elderly respondent.

Liberty to receive and visit guests

Social interaction variables are important to understand the nature and extent of abuse. Permission or liberty to receive and visit guests is one of the important social interaction variables. We have also tried to know from our respondents if their family members allow or like them to receive guests in the house, or go and visit them.

Table 4.9: Distribution of respondents having permission to receive/visit guests

Permission	*Frequency*	*Percentage*
Yes	904	90.0
No	101	10.0
Total	**1005**	**100.0**

It is revealed that an overwhelming majority of the respondents (90%) have the family members' permission to meet guests. But the remaining 10 percent of the respondents don't have permission to meet guests. It would not be incorrect to guess that these 10 percent respondents might be facing problem of abuse.

In the situation where the elderly person has no permission to meet guests and has to vacate their room, it is quite interesting to know what kind of feelings they have on the arrival of guests. It is found that majority (97.5 %) of them like arrival of guests while only 2.5 percent respondents who feel discarded very significantly. This shows a strong attitude of adjustment or accommodation among the elderly. They are not too bothered about their personal inconvenience.

Table 4.10: Distribution of respondents according to their feeling on arrival of guests

Responses	*Frequency*	*Percentage*
Feel discarded	25	2.5
Feel normal or welcome it	980	97.5
Total	**1005**	**100.0**

Care givers

The roles of care givers are very important during old age. We have tried to know from our respondents about their care takers. They have mentioned a number of relatives as their care takers (Table 4.11 and Fig. 4.1).

It is obvious from above table that main care givers to majority of male elderly are their wives (61.8%) and there daughter in laws (21.4%), while 2 female elderly majority (42.4%) of them have no body to properly take care of them. 30.1 percent female elderly's are taken care by their daughter in laws.

Table 4.11: Distribution of respondents according to their main care givers

Care giver	*Male*	*Female*
Wife	520 (61.8)	- (-)
Daughter in law	180 (21.4)	49 (30.1)
Son	30 (3.6)	18 (11.0)
Daughter	8 (0.9)	12 (7.4)
Grand son	5 (0.6)	3 (1.8)
Grand daughter	- (-)	2 (1.2)
No body	99 (11.7)	69 (42.4)
Husband	- (-)	10 (6.1)
Total	**842 (100.0)**	**163 (100.0)**

Note: Bracket indicate percentage

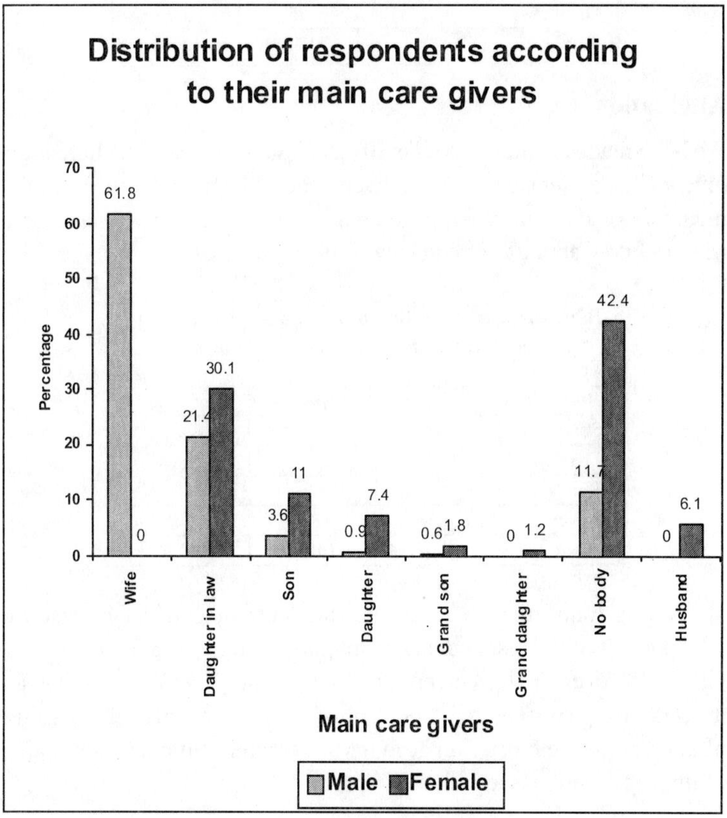

Fig. 4.1

Mixing with grand children

It is often heard especially in urban families that son or daughter- in - law don't allow their sons or daughters to interact with their grand parents. On the other side, grandparents want to take care of them and/ or pass their time with them. We got a somewhat different picture from our respondents. There is a small percent case that the sons/ daughters-in-law dislikes the elderly interacting with their children.

Table 4.12: Distribution of respondents according to sons or daughters-in-law's reaction to their mixing with their grand children

N=965

Responses	*Frequency*	*Percentage*
Like	910	94.3
Dislike	55	5.7
Total	**965**	**100.0**

Altercation

We have made an attempt to identify the issues over which altercation or conflict or tension arose between the elderly and other family members or especially with the abuser. In this regard we have first tried to know about the frequency of its prevalence.

Table 4.13: Distribution of respondents according to altercation with family members

Altercation	*Frequency*	*Percentage*
Sometimes	18	18.9
Frequently	58	5.8
Rarely	586	58.3
Never	180	17.9
Total	**1005**	**100.0**

It was found that there are no incidents of conflict in case of 17.9 percent of the respondents, in majority of cases (58.3%) it occurs rarely. However, in 18.9 percent cases some time it takes place, whereas it occurs frequently with 5.8 percent of the respondents. The reasons of altercation are mostly on account of demand of money, complaint of improper care, issues related to property, etc.

Opinion about the facilities

A large majority (73.5%) of the respondents have said in the begining that their needs are fulfilled by their children. But when we asked a question to our respondents about their opinion about the facilities provided by their families. Though most of them (94.1 percent) are satisfied with the facilities they have, still there are 5.9 percent who are dissatisfied with the available facilities to them. (See table)

Table 4.14: Distribution of respondents according to their opinion on the facilities provided to them

Opinion	*Frequency*	*Percentage*
Satisfied	946	94.1
Dissatisfied	59	5.9
Total	**1005**	**100.0**

Visit of Friends and Relatives

One of the social interaction variables is friends coming over to see them. This is an indicator of how much socially active and well connected with outside world they are. We have tried to explore this angle and came to know that majority (95.6%) of them are privileged as their friends visits them off and on.

Table 4.15: Distribution of respondents according to their friends coming over to them

Friends' visit	*Frequency*	*Percentage*
Yes	961	95.6
No	44	4.4
Total	**1005**	**100.0**

Only 4.4 percent of the respondents say that their friends don't come to meet them. To conclude, we may say that except this minority, very large majority of the respondents enjoy the privilege of having their friend visiting them.

It is quite interesting and important to know that almost cent percent respondents' relatives do come to visit them. However, only a few (5.9 percent) visit frequently. 51.4 percent respondent's relatives come sometimes and 42.7 percent respondents' friends and relatives visit them rarely.

Visit to Friends House

Only this is not important that their friends are visiting them, but whether they are also going to friends' houses at times is also very important. It is found that a majority (52.2%) of them visit friends' house occasionally; 34.1 percent rarely go out to visit friends and 9.3 percent respondents visit friends' houses frequently. It is only 4.4 percent respondents who never go to their friends' houses. They happen to be the same respondents whom no friend visits.

Table 4.16: Distribution of respondents according to their visits to friends' house

Visits	*Frequency*	*Percentage*
Frequently	93	9.3
Occasionally	525	52.2
Rarely	343	34.1
Never	44	4.4
Total	**1005**	**100.0**

Hospitality to Friends

It is a very good sign of healthy social interaction that elderly respondents are going to their friends' house and their friends too are visiting them. But whether their friends are getting due hospitality from the family members of the respondents, is also very important to know as one of the indicators of the status of the elderly in the family. We find that almost all (95.8%) the respondents' friends get proper hospitality on their visits.

Table 4.17: Distribution of respondents according to due hospitality to their friends

N= 961

Due Hospitality	*Frequency*	*Percentage*
Yes	921	95.8
No	40	4.2
Total	**961**	**100.0**

As shown above 4.2 percent respondents have revealed that their friends are not given any, or proper hospitality by the family members when they come to visit them. It shows the status of elderly persons, and that they themselves are being neglected by their families, in the same manner as their friends.

Relations with Neighbours

A cordial relationship with the neighbours is a source of several types of helps and protection at the time of crisis or emergency. We have explored our respondents' relations with their neighbors. We have found that 9.3 percent of the respondents' relations with their neighbor are cordial, 9.7 percent respondents' relations are not cordial, and 74.1 percent respondents normal and remaining 6.9 percent have no relations with them at all.

Table 4.18: Distribution of respondents according to their relationship with neighbors

Relations	*Frequency*	*Percentage*
Cordial	93	9.3
Not cordial	98	9.7
Normal	745	74.1
No relations at all	69	6.9
Total	**1005**	**100.0**

The above data shows that majority of the respondents have normal relations with their neighbors' but about 16.6 percent respondents are also there whose relations with their neighbours are not cordial or just non-existent.

Accompanying them to Religious / Tourist Places

In old age, it is very difficult, and to some extent not even impossible for any elderly person to move out of his residence to attend any socio-religious functions and travel to any tourist place. There is a difference between going alone and going along with family members, which reflects the caring nature of family. The response of our respondents in this regard is presented in the following table.

Table 4.19: Distribution of respondents according to their family members taking them to social and/or religious ceremonies, tourist places

Response	*Frequency*	*Percentage*
Yes	848	84.4
No	157	15.6
Total	**1005**	**100.0**

It is obvious from the above table that a large majority (84.4%) of the respondents enjoys this privileges but a significant number of respondents (15.6%) are not so fortunate to have their family members accompanying them to religious/tourist places. It is important to know the reasons for the family members not taking them on such visits. The reasons given by the respondents are presented in the following table.

Table 4.20: Distribution of respondents according to the reasons for family for not taking them to socio-religious ceremonies and tourist places

N= 157

Reasons	*Frequency*	*Percentage*
Because of advanced old age	56	35.7
Due to neglect	40	25.5
Own disinterestedness	55	35.0
Economic crisis	6	3.8
Total	**157**	**100.0**

According to the respondents the reason for not taking them to socio-religious functions or tourist places is that they are themselves (35.0 percent) not interested to go, while significant number (35.7%) of respondents feel that it is because they have become too old for outside travel,. 3.8 percent has mentioned the reason as economic crises. Further, it is important to note that at least 25.5 percent have charged that it is due to neglect on the part of their family members.

Change in Respect

Due to several reasons family values are changing. The status of older persons is not the same as it was earlier. They are not enjoying same prestige and honor as the elderly used to enjoy in the past. We have tried to explore from the respondents whether they are getting same respect as it was earlier. The responses are presented in the following table.

Table 4.21: Distribution of respondents according to change in status

Respect received	*Frequency*	*Percentage*
Same	711	70.7
Relatively less	294	29.3
Total	**1005**	**100.0**

A large majority of the respondents (70.7%) say that they are enjoying the same respect as earlier, while 29.3 percent respondents feel that they are not enjoying the same amount of respect. To conclude, we may say that this proves a significant proportion of elderly population have experienced a decline in the respect within their families.

Table 4.22: Distribution of respondents according to reasons of elderly persons' neglect and loss of respect

Reasons	*Percentage**
Changed family values	95.0
Selfish attitude of family members	81.0
Dependency of elderly	48.0
Dual career family	52.0
Lack of time with caregivers	70.0
Financial hardship	10.0

* Multiple responses

Several reasons have been mentioned for the change in status by our respondents. According to them the main reasons are changing family values (95%) selfish attitude (81%), and lack of time with care givers (70%), dual career family (52%), dependency of elderly (48.0 %) and financial hardship (10.0 %).

Disintegration of joint family has significantly affected the status of the aged persons. Traditionally joint family provided care and security to the aged persons.

We asked a question to our respondents if they agreed that disintegration of joint family is the reason for neglect and abuse of the elderly. Their responses are presented in the following table.

Table 4.23: Distribution of respondents according to their views on disintegration of joint family as the main reason for neglect and abuse of the elderly

Response	*Frequency*	*Percentage*
Yes	986	98.1
No	19	1.9
Total	**1005**	**100.0**

It is found that the respondents (98.1%) almost unanimously agree that neglect and abuse of elderly is mainly due to disintegration of joint family. Only 1.9 percent respondents disagreed with this view .To conclude, we may say that almost all the respondents have reasoned disintegration of joint family as the cause of neglect of the elderly.

Sharing Domestic Chores

We have tried to know the extent to which our respondents are sharing domestic chores. A very large majority of the respondents (92.2%) do participate in domestic chores, while 7.8 percent of them said no, they don't participate in it. To conclude, we may say that generally all elderly people participate in domestic chores.

Table 4.24: Distribution of respondents according to their participation in domestic work

Help in domestic work	*Frequency*	*Percentage*
Yes	927	92.2
No	78	7.8
Total	**1005**	**100.0**

Almost all the family members have to do one or other types of domestic chores. After retirement from work, aged people keep them engage by doing domestic work of their liking. In some families they do this not voluntarily but due to compulsion.

Our respondents have also mentioned several types of domestic chores that they perform. Nature of work is quite different amongst urban and rural elderly. Only 5 percent of our respondents have revealed that they have to do it under pressure as they don't have a liking to do such work and also their age doesn't permit taking strain.

Table 4.25: Distribution of respondents according to performed nature of domestic chores

N=927*

Domestic chores	*Percentage*
Bringing milk	31.0
Bringing vegetables & fruits, grocery	38.5
Help in house cleaning	11.0
Drinking water management	16.0
Giving fodder to animals	18.0
Milking cows/buffalos	9.0
Dropping and bringing back kids from school	16.0
Cooking as and when required	4.0
Bringing fire wood for cooking	9.0
Watering of plants	38.8
Taking care of pet animals	27.0
Bill payments	28.0
Taking care of kids	27.0
Teaching grand sons/daughters	22.0
Attending visitors/guests	40.0
House watch & ward	59.7

* Multiple answers

We have received multiple responses to the question on nature of domestic work performed by the respondents. It is quite interesting to note that a large majority (59.7%) of the respondents have said that they do watch and ward of their houses. Not only in the absence of the family members but also in the presence of all they have to take care of the general security and supervision. The other most important work is to attend guests and visitors (40%). 38.8 percent of the respondents do watering of plants, 38.5 percent respondents bring vegetables, fruits and grocery from the market, 31 percent bring milk, 28 percent respondents go for the payment of different bills (like telephone, electricity, house tax, water tax etc), 27 percent respondents take care of animals and also of kids, they teach them (22%), do the work of dropping and bringing them from schools (16%), collect fodder (18%) for animals, store drinking water (16%), help in house cleaning (11 %), collecting fuel wood for cooking etc. It is clear from the above table that our respondents perform almost all sorts of domestic work, which should be helpful for them to keep fit and busy and also enhance their value and esteem in the family.

Availability of Services of Servants

During old age proper care is required. It will be of great help to them if an elderly have the services of a servant. In the present time in the family no body has spare time to properly look after the elderly person or persons. Some elderly especially the oldest-old or otherwise disabled require almost full time care. Generally, family members don't understand this requirement of elderly members. They don't hire a servant due to two reasons, one, in many cases sheer selfishness and second, in most of the cases due to economic reasons. However, trained servants are also not available to take proper care of elderly persons.

We inquired about the availability of services of servants to our respondents. Evidently, only a few (2.9%) respondents have a servant to take care of them. On the contrary, 97.1 percent have to manage without a helper or servant. This appears to be strange because economic status-wise as a large proportion of the families can afford hiring helper to take care of their elderly (see table 4.26).

Table 4.26: Distribution of respondents according to provision of a servant to take care of them

Having a servant	*Frequency*	*Percentage*
Yes	30	2.9
No	975	97.1
Total	**1005**	**100.0**

Feeling of Neglect

Now days it is a common fact that an elderly person experiences some or the other form of abuse from one or the other member of the family. Neglect is one of the most dangerous forms of psychological abuse. It is as fatal as any other type of abuse.

We have tried to know from our respondents if they are experiencing neglect by their family members. The data is presented in the following table.

Table 4.27: Distribution of respondents according to their feeling of neglect

If feeling neglected?	*Frequency*	*Percentage*
Yes	463	46.1
No	542	53.9
Total	**1005**	**100.0**

It is obvious from the above table that 46.1 percent in of the respondents have revealed that they do feel neglected, while majority of the respondents (53.9 percent) has said that they don't have any such feeling. On collecting this relevant data we find that the respondents who are not experiencing neglect by their family members are either the main earners or are in the category of young- old or/and also member of prosperous joint family.

Unhappiness with Family Member

We have tried to know from our respondents about their unhappiness with any of the family member, just to get some idea about elder abuse. It is revealed that 27.1 percent respondents were found unhappy with some or other members of the family. In comparison to male (26.0%) more females (32.5%) are unhappy with one or other member of the family (See table below).

Table 4.28: Distribution of respondents according to their unhappiness

Response	*Male*	*Female*	*Total*
Yes	219 (26.0)	53 (32.5)	272 (27.1)
No	623 (74.0)	110 (67.5)	733 (72.9)
Total	**842 (83.8)**	**163 (16.2)**	**1005 (100.0)**

Note: Figures in the brackets denotes Percentage

27.1 percent respondents who are unhappy with their family member/s has stated further about the particular member with whom they are unhappy. It is found that majority of male respondents (85.5%), and a large majority of female respondents (79.2%) are unhappy with their daughters-in-law. It is interesting to know that 16.0 percent of male respondents are unhappy with their wives and 18.9 percent female respondents are unhappy with their husbands.

Table 4.29: Distribution of respondents according to their unhappiness with family members

Relation	*Male (N=219)*	*Female (N=53)*
Wife	35 (16.0)	- (-)
Daughter-in-law	188 (85.8)	42 (79.2)
Son	52 (23.7)	18 (34.0)
Husband	- (-)	10 (18.9)
Brother's Wife	- (-)	02 (3.8)
Grand Son	04 (1.8)	- (-)

* Some of the respondents are unhappy with more than one members of the family.

It is also important to know the reasons of unhappiness. Since a significant number, that is 27.1 percent respondents were unhappy with one or the other members of the family. We, therefore, tried to explore various reasons of their unhappiness. The respondents have revealed several reasons which are presented in the following table.

Table 4.30: Distribution of respondents according to reasons of unhappiness

N=272*

Reasons	*Frequency*	*Percentage*
Don't respect	125	45.9
Create tension/problem	170	62.5
Don't adjust	130	47.8
Don't obey	112	41.2
Selfish attitude	180	66.2
Don't take proper care	135	49.6

* Multiple responses

It is obvious from the above table that the main reason (66.2 %) of unhappiness is selfish attitude of a particular member (mostly of daughter-in-law and son) and also members creating tension or problems (62.5%) on several occasions. The other reasons of unhappiness are improper care (49.3%), not adjusting properly (47.8%) with other family members, not paying due respect (45.9%) and also not obeying (41.2%).

To conclude, we may say that respondents are mostly unhappy with their family members because of their selfish attitude and tendency of creating tensions in the family.

Staying in Old Age Home

As regard the very idea of staying in Old Age Home (OAH) during old age, though majority (81.6 percent) of the respondents were against it, yet not an insignificant, that is 18.4 percent of them were not averse to staying in Old Age Homes. On case to case analysis we find that most of those respondents who were those who also were victims of abuse. A few religious minded respondents were also favoured OAH.

Table 4.31: Distribution of respondents according to their views on staying at Old Age Home

Responses	*Frequency*	*Percentage*
Yes	185	18.4
No	820	81.6
Total	**1005**	**100.0**

Thus, 18.4 percent respondents were found to be in favour of OAH, but when we asked them about their likely possibility of staying in OAH, it was found that only 56.8 percent of them answered in favour of that. To conclude, we may say that generally elderly people still prefer to stay with their families.

Table 4.32: Distribution of respondents according to their liking to stay in old age homes

N=185

Response	*Frequency*	*Percentage*
Yes	105	56.8
No	80	43.2
Total	**185**	**100.0**

Social Isolation and Feeling of Loneliness

The feeling of loneliness and psychological isolation and unhelpful attitude by other members of family do contribute to negative influence on elderly people's well being. (A. Venkoba Rao, 1996:45) We have also tried to know from our respondents about social isolation and the feelings of loneliness experienced by them. As an indicator of social isolation we have chosen the duration of remaining alone by our elderly respondents. As of isolation, we have classified our respondents into four categories- (a) highly isolated- who remain alone for more than 8 hours in a day. (b) Moderately isolated-who remain alone for 4 to 8 hours in a day. (c) Least isolated-who remain alone for less than 4 hours in a day.

It was found that a vast majority (84.0%) of male and female (71.7%) respondents reported that they never felt isolated.However,2.9 percent male and 7.4 percent female respondents were found highly isolated, while 2.4 percent male and 2.5 percent female moderately and remaining 10.7 percent male and 18.4 percent female respondents least isolated.

With regard to feeling of loneliness, as experienced by respondents, it was found that 7.4 percent male and 8.6 percent female always had a feeling of loneliness while 11.9 percent male and 17.8 percent female sometime feel loneliness.

Table 4.33: Extent of isolation and loneliness among the respondents

	Male (N=842)	*Female (N=163)*
Extent of Isolation-		
Highly isolated	25 (2.9)	12 (7.4)
Moderately isolated	20 (2.4)	04 (2.5)
Least isolated	90 (10.7)	30 (18.4)
Not isolated	707 (84.0)	117 (71.7)
Feeling of Loneliness-		
Always	62 (7.4)	14 (8.6)
Sometimes	100 (11.9)	29 (17.8)
Never	680 (80.7)	120 (73.6)

Views on Old Age

Ageing is a natural phenomenon and every living thing is subjected to this phenomenon. Each individual has to prepare him or herself for the effects of time. But due to biological ageing and several other factors people find it difficult to cope with the inevitable changes in their body, family relations and social adjustment etc. Therefore, we have also tried to know from our respondents what they think of this stage of life. Their responses are presented in the following table.

Table 4.34: Distribution of respondents according to their views on old age

Perception	***Frequency***	***Percentage***
Difficult/painful	690	68.7
It's natural	315	31.3
Total	**1005**	**100.0**

It is obvious from the above table that majority (68.7 %) of the respondents said that old age is the most painful stage of life, while 31.3 percent respondents did not think so. To conclude, we may say that majority (68.7%) of the respondents thought that this was the most painful stage of life.

With advancing age, death is round the corner. People know this fact that their body is destructible. Despite of this fear of death haunts their minds. Thus the fear of death mars their happiness. Keeping this fact in view, we have also tried to know from our respondents if they are also worried by the fear of death. It was found that a large majority (71.6%) of them accepted that they have fear of death. It is very interesting to know that large numbers (49.1%) of female respondents are less afraid of death in comparison to male respondents (24.3%). The reason of their being less afraid of death might be due to their lesser stake in life.

Table 4.35: Distribution of respondents according to fear of death

If afraid of death?	***Male***	***Female***	***Total***
Yes	637 (75.7)	83 (50.9)	720 (71.6)
No	205 (24.3)	80 (49.1)	285 (28.4)
Total	**842 (83.8)**	**163 (16.2)**	**1005 (100.0)**

It is often said that with age behavior of a man changes. Our respondents are also of the same view, wherein majority of them (79.0%) have said that they realize that there is a change in their behavior.

Table 4.36: Distribution of respondents according to their realization of behavioral changes

If behavioral changes any ?	*Frequency*	*Percent*
Yes	794	79.0
No	211	21.0
Total	**1005**	**100.0**

Leisure Time Activities

Leisure is important in life. For working people availability of leisure time is a problem, but for elderly people especially those who have withdrawn from active engagement it is not a problem. For them problem is to how to pass time. People spend their leisure time differently. According to Havinghurst (1960:903) how one uses his time depends on his personality. On the other hand according to Thompson and Streib (1960) it depends on ones relationships in society. In order to know what keeps the aged persons busy or in what sort of leisure time activities the aged are mainly engaged in, responses were obtained from them about their main activity of leisure time.

Table 4.37: Distribution of respondents according to their leisure-time activity

N=1005*

Leisure-time activity	*Frequency*	*Percentage*
Reading news papers/magazines	610	60.7
Kirtan Bhajan/worship	340	33.8
Radio listening	280	27.9
T.V. watching	740	73.6
Playing cards	70	6.9
Morning/Evening walk	418	41.6
Kitchen gardening	205	20.4
Social Work	95	9.4
Political work	165	16.4
Gossiping/chatting	270	26.7
Tending animals	20	2.0

*Multiple responses

It is found that the percentage of elderly people who watch T.V. is highest (73.6%). Besides T.V. news papers play an important role for the elderly as 60.7 percent of them like to read newspapers/magazines daily. While elderly women watch T.V. more than men the elderly men read more newspaper than women. The availability of T.V. is less in rural areas hence several respondents don't watch television. 41.6 percent respondents go for walk; 33.8 percent respondent's hobbies are chanting bhajan- Kirtan and visiting worship places. 26.7 percent enjoy in gossiping and chatting with friends and others. Likewise 27.9 percent respondent's hobby is to listen radio. Majority of the radio listeners are from rural areas, where radio is still popular because of less availability of T.V. and electricity too. Some of the respondents (20.4%) do kitchen gardening, some (16.4%) political and social work (9.4%) and some (2.0%) tending animals. To conclude, we may say that watching T.V. and reading news papers/magazines are the two most popular leisure-time activities of elderly respondents.

Upkeep of Pet Animals

In old age keeping pet animals could be a creatively useful hobby. It would not only keep them busy but also require them to do physical activity. Besides, pets would be a big source of avoiding loneliness. In our country generally people don't understand the importance of pet animals especially their positive role in lessening the depression in the lives of the elderly.

Table 4.38: Distribution of respondents according to upkeep of pet animals

Pet animals	*Frequency*	*Percentage*
Yes	401	39.9
No	604	60.1
Total	**1005**	**100.0**

It is clear from the above table that though majority (60.1%) of the respondent doesn't have pet animals, a large number (39.9%) of respondents do have pet animals in their homes. These pet animals include cow, buffalo, goat and dog. Some of the respondents' have some other animals and birds like hen, cock, pigeon, sheep etc. Majority of the respondents (89.5%) accepted that due to these pet animals they get some respite from loneliness. The remaining respondents (60.1%) who don't have pet animals, on being asked about their wish to have any pet animal, only a few (10%) said that they wanted to keep them but circumstance are not favorable to do so.

Needless to say that keeping dairy cattle's, goat, sheep etc. is part of the rural life and so of the respondents living in rural areas. These may not be of austenitic value or recreation of them.

Chapter - 5

Health Status

It is a fact that due to several reasons longevity is increasing. It is worth if health is good but it is unfortunate that many Indian elderly persons often suffer from one or the other disease and are not free from disability.

Wan (1982) conceptualizes health as a state of well-being measured by subjective assessment of overall health and life satisfaction, and by physical functional capacities of the older adults. (Wan, Thomas, T.H. (1982), Stressful Life Events, Social Support Networks and Gerontological Health, Lexington: Lexington Books). But, here in this chapter under health status we have described prevalence of diseases and health care related issues only. The purpose is to know the incidence of elder abuse due to health problems and medical needs of the elderly.

There are several studies which have shown relationship between age and decline in health status (for example see Burton and Zimmerman, 1986; Williams, 1984; Kyiatkos et al. 1984). Several socio-economic characteristics like living arrangements, quality of life, marital status, financial status etc determine health status of an elderly. (Ramamurti and Jamuna, 1992; Kathy and Carson, 1992; Palmore, 1986 etc).

Ageing is a biological process which gradually damages the organism and reduces its viability. With advancing age, physical deterioration and decrease in vitality, the elderly exhibit greater vulnerability towards diseases. (Hebibullah, C.M. 1996). There is a close connection between ageing and some diseases from which an elderly suffers. It is important to mention here that old age is not a disease in itself. There arise several common old age health problems and diseases, like high or low blood pressure, heart problems, gout, arthritis, spondylitis, respiratory diseases, enlargement of prostate, other type of genitor-urinary disorders, loss of teeth, eye diseases, hearing defects, dental problems, cancer, paralysis, Alzheimer, dementia, piles, fistula and gynecological problems and so on . In our country providing medical care to an elderly is a big problem especially for the poor elderly. The health needs of the aged often go unattended due to neglect and lack of care and of course sometime due to other reasons too, e.g. financial affordability, access to health care practices and so on.

Incidence of diseases

Elder abuse is also directly or indirectly linked with the health status of the elderly person. If an aged person is suffering from some chronic disease he will put not only financial burden on family but seek more care. The increased socio-economic pressure due to ill health may lead to one or other type of abuse.

Keeping in view of this we have tried to know the incidence of diseases among our respondents. It was found that majority of our respondents (91.3%) are suffering from several types of diseases which have been presented in the table 5.1 and Fig. 5.1.

Table 5.1: Distribution of respondents according to incidence of diseases

N= 918

Disease	*Percentage*
Urinal Problem/enlarge prostate	32.1
Cataract, Glaucoma and retinal disorder	69.0
Hearing defects	11.0
Problems related to digestion or low apatite	31.0
General Weakness or debility	52.5
Joint pains or Arthritis	39.5
Asthma or similar problems (respiratory problem)	20.4
Low/High Blood Pressure	65.2
Dental problem	56.2
Kidney related problems	2.1
Heart related problems	7.8

(Contd...)

Paralysis	1.0
Cancer	1.0
Poor memory, Initial stage of Dementia/Alzheimer	13.0
Vertigo (Ghumta)	29.0
Diabetes	32.0
Gynecological problems (only to females)	22.0
Piles, Fistula etc.	27.0

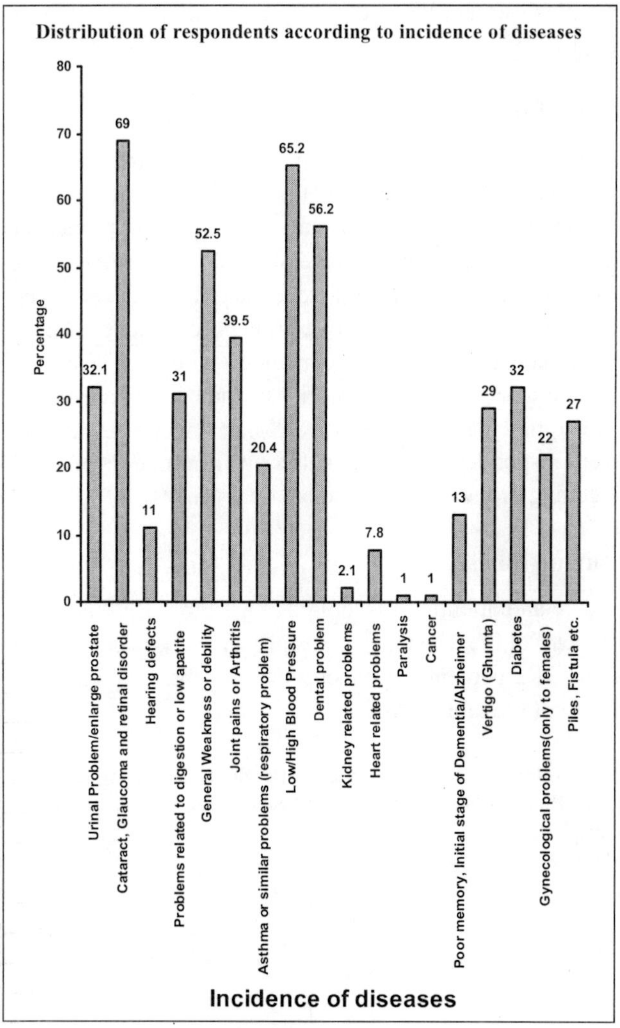

Fig. 5.1

Disease wise analysis clearly shows that majority of the respondents are suffering from the problem of low or high blood pressure (65.2%), cataract, Glaucoma and retinal disorders (69.0%), dental problem (56.2%), diabetes (32.0%), joint pains, gouts or arthritis (39.5%), vertigo (Ghumta) (29.0%), enlargement of prostate and urinal problems (32.1%), problems of piles and/ or fistula (27.0%) and general weakness (52.5%) etc. Furthermore, some of the respondents are also suffering from chronic diseases like cancer (1.0%) and initial stage of Dementia/ Alzheimer (13.0%).

Problems of proper treatment

The nature of health problems reported would need both preventive and curative care to be provided to the affected elderly persons. Cent percent respondents said that it is very difficult to get proper medical treatment. They have mentioned several problems associated with their treatment. About 60 percent respondent said that it is very expensive and also not easy for an elderly person to consult doctors. Their movement depends on the family member/ caregiver. Not that good hospitals are a few only, the majority of the doctors are not serious about attending elderly patients (59.7%). It is worth mentioning that 22 percent respondents who are suffering from one or other disease are not getting proper regular medical treatment.

Care during illness

Special care and attention is required at the time of illness. Majority (68.8 percent) of the respondents gets proper attention and care during illness, but 31.2 percent respondents are also there who are deprived of such care. (See table below)

Table 5.2: Distribution of respondents according to facility of proper attention and care at the time of illness

Response	*Frequency*	*Percentage*
Yes	691	68.8
No	314	31.2
Total	**1005**	**100.0**

In time availability of medicine

Availability of medicine in time is very important in old age. Generally an older person needs a family member's support to have medicine in time. 69.2 percent of our respondents have said that they get medicine in time whenever they fell ill, while 30.8 percent respondent has said it is not available to them in time. To conclude, we may say that though at the time of illness majority of them get medicines in time, however close to one-third of the respondents are not getting their medicines in time is quite alarming.

Table 5.3: Distribution of respondents according to timely serving of medicines

Timely Medicine	*Frequency*	*Percentage*
Yes	695	69.2
No	310	30.8
Total	**1005**	**100.0**

Symptoms of depression

Many changes occur due to aging which can be physical, physiological, cognitive, and social or often a combination of these four major syndromes. Ageing affects almost all processes of life and depression can be a consequence of any one or multiple of these changes. (Sahani Bhogle and Revati Reddy, 1996:178). It was found that depression is the common psychiatric disorder in the later years of life.

On the basis of prominent physical signs i.e. loss of appetite, weight loss, fatigue especially in the morning, sleeplessness, constipation and the like and also along with these some of the associative symptoms like tension, anxiety, tremulousness, agitation, guilt feeling and crying in some cases, we have observed symptoms of mild depression among 31.1 percent respondents.

Table 5.4: Distribution of respondents according to frequent feeling tension or some form of depression

Response	*Frequency*	*Percentage*
Yes	313	31.1
No	692	68.9
Total	**1005**	**100.0**

It is quite alarming that 65.1 percent respondents said that due to their illness their children/family members pay less attention to taking care of them, they even consider them as burdensome.

Table 5.5: Distribution of respondents according to their feeling about care and attention given by family members

N=918

Response	*Frequency*	*Percentage*
Attention, care lacking, consider burdensome	598	65.1
Feel good	320	34.9
Total	**918**	**100.0**

Regular medical checkup

During old age regular medical check up is advisable. But due to lack of easy access to proper medical and health facilities it is not possible by many, especially the older people, who live in remote rural areas.

Majority (74.1%) of the respondents don't go for the regular medical check up. The inability to have regular medical check- up could be either due to lack of access to medical facilities or just because of their ignorance about its importance. It is also interesting to know that not a single elderly female respondent regularly goes for medical checkup.

Table 5.6: Distribution of respondents according to status about regular medical checkup

Medical Checkup	*Frequency*	*Percentage*
Regular	260	25.9
Irregular or none	745	74.1
Total	**1005**	**100.0**

We have further explored from our respondents who are having regular medical checkup, the place of their medical examination. It is found that near majority respondents (46.2%) visit private doctor for such checkups.

Table No.5.7: Distribution of respondents according to place of regular medical checkup

N=260

Place of check up	*Frequency*	*Percentage*
Private Allopath	120	46.2
Govt. Hospital	78	30.0
Private Hospital	60	23.1
Aayurvedic Doctor	2	0.7
Total	**260**	**100.0**

We have also tried to explore from our respondents who don't go for regular medical checkups, the reasons there of. A very large majority (59.7%) of the respondents said that doctors are not attentive. They don't give proper attention to aged patients. On the other hand 52.3 percent said that medical checkups is very expensive, while 29.5 percent respondents have said that it is difficult to go for medical checkups as someone is required to accompany them and also problem of conveyance also comes very often. 21.5 percent respondents have said that it is because hospitals are very far away from their residence (Table 5.8 and Fig. 5.2).

Table 5.8: Distribution of respondents according to their reasons for not having regular medical checkups

N=745*

Reasons	*Frequency*	*Percentage*
Hospitals are far away	160	21.5
Doctors are not attentive	445	59.7
Difficult to go	220	29.5
Very expensive	390	52.3

*Multiple answers

Bearer of medical expenses

It is also very important to know who bears the medical expenses of an elderly persons in the family. In this regard we have collected information from all the respondents including those who (total 87) have earlier reported to us that they are not suffering from any diseases. It was revealed that majority of the male respondents (47.5%) bear their medical expenses by themselves, while the medical expenses of

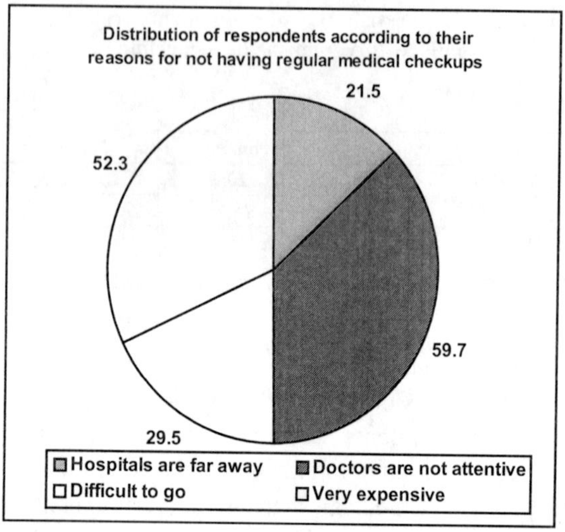

Fig. 5.2

majority (38.0%) of the female respondents are borne by their husband. In the case of 44.2 percent male respondents and 30.7 percent female respondents medical expenses are borne by their sons. Overall, we find that a near majority (43.9%) of the respondents bear medical expenses by themselves, followed by those (42.0%) whose expenses are met by their sons.

Table 5.9: Distribution of respondents according to the bearer of their medical expenses

Borne by	*Male*	*Female*	*Total*
Self	400 (47.5)	41 (25.2)	441 (43.9)
Son	372 (44.2)	50 (30.7)	422 (42.0)
Husband	-	62 (38.0)	62 (6.2)
Wife	41 (4.9)	-	41 (4.1)
Others	29 (3.4)	10 (6.1)	39 (3.8)
Total	**842 (83.8)**	**163 (16.2)**	**1005 (100.0)**

Ability to perform daily routine

With advancing old age or due to certain disabilities one finds it difficult to do his daily routine by himself. The oldest-old or disabled need some help for this.

It was revealed that majority (90.2%) of the respondents doesn't have such problem but there are a few (9.8%) who have problem in doing daily routine.

Table 5.10: Distribution of respondents according to ability to perform their daily routine

If difficulty faced?	*Frequency*	*Percentage*
Yes	98	9.8
No	907	90.2
Total	**1005**	**100.0**

Now question comes that who helps those 9.8 percent elderly respondents in performing of their daily routine. It was revealed that majority (29.1%) of the male respondents gets help for doing their daily routine by their daughters-in-law. However, 16.3 percent get help from their sons, 14 percent from their grand son, 11.6 percent from their wives 2.3 percent from servants and remaining 26.7 percent don't get help from any one. When we compare this with female respondents 25.0 percent of them don't get help from anyone. 25 percent women get help from their sons and other 25 percent from their husbands, 16.7 percent of them get help from their daughters-in-laws and remaining 8.3 percent from their granddaughters. To conclude, we may say that almost majority (26.5%) of the elderly respondents don't get any help in their daily routine. One can understand their problem easily.

Table 5.11: Distribution of respondents according to care givers in performing daily routine

N=98

Caregiver	*Male (n=86)*	*Female (n=12)*
Son	14 (16.3)	3 (25.0)
Daughter-in-Law	25 (29.1)	2 (16.7)
Wife	10 (11.6)	-
Husband	-	3 (25.0)
Grandson/daughter	12 (14.0)	1 (8.3)
Servant	2 (2.3)	-
None	23 (26.7)	3 (25.0)

Habits

In eastern Uttar Pradesh and especially in Varanasi chewing paan and chewing khaini (tobacco) are very common. Varanasi is famous for thandai also (with or without bhang). gutka (tobacco) consumption is also very high. Some lower class/caste people enjoy ganja also. Naturally we tried to find its prevalence among our respondents (see table below).

Table 5.12: Distribution of the respondents according to their habits*

Habits	*Male (N=760)*	*Female (N=68)*
Chewing Pann with tobacco	490 (64.5)	25 (36.8)
Eating Khaini	410 (53.9)	35 (51.5)
Gutka	395 (51.9)	15 (22.1)
Smoking (cigerate,biri)	385 (50.6)	10 (14.7)
Alcohol use (CML or FML)	290 (38.1)	2 (2.9)
Bhaang	110 (14.5)	- (0.0)
Smoking Ganja	58 (7.6)	- (0.0)

* Multiple responses

When we enquired from our respondents about their habits of drinking alcohol or chewing paan etc., we found that maximum number of respondents (64.5% male and 36.8% female) do chew paan with tobacco followed by those who take khaini (53.9% male and 51.5% female) and Gutka (51.9% male and 22.1% female), Cigarettes smoking (mostly in urban areas) or Biri (in rural areas) (50.6 %male and 14.7% female), drinking alcohol (Desi/country made liquor-CML) by poor people, mainly in rural areas and India made foreign liquor (IMFL) by rich and urban (higher class) people. (38.1% male and 2.9% female). The habit of taking 'Bhang' is also found amongst some (14.5%) of our male respondents. A few male respondents (7.6%) also admitted that they sometimes do enjoy smoking Ganja.

Among elderly female respondents, majority (51.5%) eats Khaini followed by those chewing paan with tobacco (36.8%) and eating Gutka (22.1%), Biri smoking (14.7%) and a few lower caste female (2.9%) do take desi liquor (CML) on some occasions. The respondents were very largely untouched by the ban on tobacco products. They also were not conscious of any ill effects of these habits on their health. This apparently calls for an intensive awareness campaign focused on the elderly population.

Chapter - 6

Economic Status & Abuse

In this chapter we have analyzed data about the elderly respondent's own income, sources of income, dependency, their family income, assets and debts, earner and dependent members and litigation on property matters, abuse etc.

Own Income

As regards individual monthly income of the respondents, we find that 19.4 percent respondents have no income at all, followed by around 48 percent having an income of up to Rs. 5000/- per month, 13.9 percent having income of Rs. 5001 to 10,000/-, 10.5 percent between Rs. 10001 to Rs. 15000/-, 5 percent between Rs. 15001 to Rs. 20000 and remaining 3.4 percent respondents income is Rs. 20001 or more than that. The respondents whose income is more than Rs. 15000/- per month are mostly from urban areas and that too mostly pensioners.

Sex-wise distribution of monthly income of the respondents clearly shows that majority (52.1%) of the female respondents have no income of their own; they would have been categorized as 'house wife' (See Table 6.1 and Fig. 6.1).

Table 6.1: Distribution of respondents according to their monthly income (from all sources)

Monthly family income (in Rs.)	*Male*	*Female*	*Total*
No Income	110 (13.1)	85 (52.1)	195 (19.4)
Less than 5000	421 (50.0)	59 (36.2)	480 (47.8)

(*Contd...*)

5001 to 10000	135 (16.0)	5 (3.1)	140 (13.9)
10001 to 15000	98 (11.6)	8 (4.9)	106 (10.5)
15001 to 20000	46 (5.5)	4 (2.5)	50 (5.0)
20,001	32 (3.8)	2 (1.2)	34 (3.4)
Total	**842 (83.8)**	**163 (16.2)**	**1005 (100.0)**

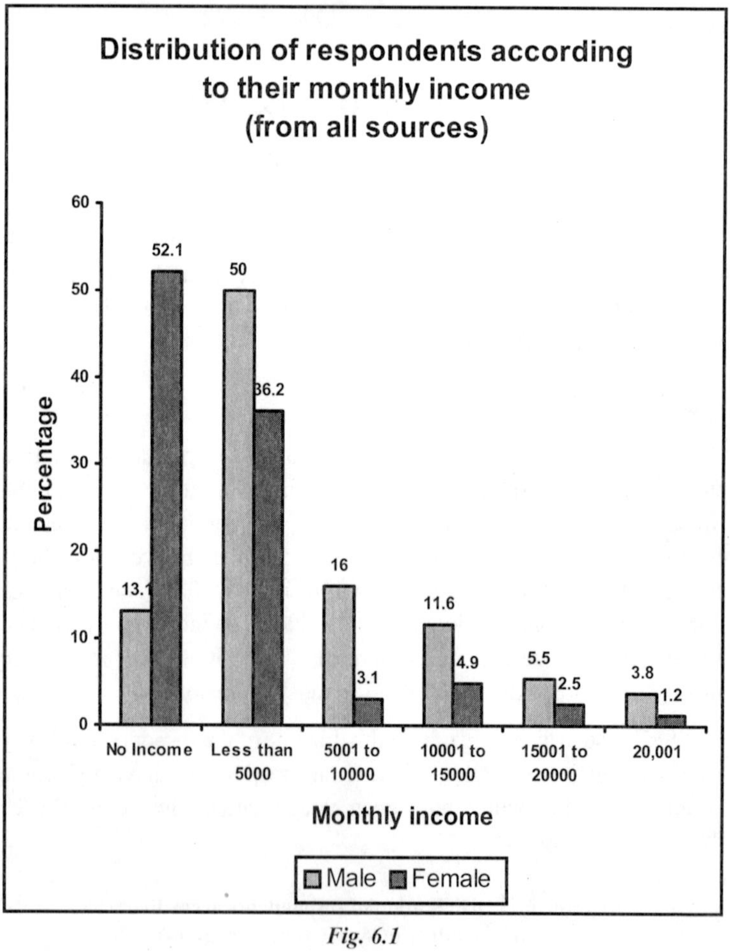

Fig. 6.1

Sources of Income

As regards the respondents' sources of income, we have come to know that they have various sources of income. However 19.4 percent of them have no source of income and they are totally dependent on family members or others. The main sources of income are: rental income (32.3%), income from agriculture (30.8%), and service pension (12.7%), 9.7 percent Social Security Old Age Pension/Widow Pension, 1.3 percent earn their income through professional practice, 6.3 percent from petty business and 8.4 percent from other sources. It is important to note that 16.6 percent respondents earn their income from wage labor, which implies that though their old age may not allow hard work they are still working for their survival and that too with physical labor. This class should be the primary concern of the policy planners.

Table 6.2: Distribution of respondents according to sources of income

N= 1005*

Sl. No.	*Sources of Income*	*Frequency*	*Per cent*
1.	Pension	128	12.7
2.	Rental Income	325	32.3
3.	Old Age Pension/Widow Pension	98	9.7
4.	Income from agriculture	310	30.8
5.	Petty Business	64	6.3
6.	Wages	167	16.6
7.	Professional practice	14	1.3
8.	Other sources	85	8.4
9.	No Source of Income	195	19.4

*Respondents have mentioned multiple sources of income.

Family Income

In addition to the respondent's personal monthly income, it is important to know the total monthly family income of the respondents. It was revealed that nearly 68 percent respondents' family fell in the monthly income range of Rs. 10,000/- or less than that, followed by nearly 32 percent respondents having family income of Rs. 10,000/- or more than that. It is important to note that 0.8 percent respondent's family income is nil, it means they are fully dependent on relatives or neighbors.

Sex-wise distribution of family income clearly shows that majority of female respondents' (54.6%) monthly family income is less than 5000Rs. In comparison to male counterparts (7.5%) only, 3.7 percent female respondent's family income is more than Rs.20,000 per month (Table 6.3 and Fig. 6.2).

Table 6.3: Distribution of respondents according to their monthly family income

Monthly family income (in Rs.)	*Male*	*Female*	*Total*
Nil	5 (0.6)	3 (1.8)	8 (0.8)
Up to 5000	240 (28.5)	86 (52.8)	326 (32.4)
5001-10,000	325 (38.6)	30 (18.4)	355 (35.3)
10,001-15,000	122 (14.5)	20 (12.3)	142 (14.1)
15001-20,000	87 (10.3)	18 (11.0)	105 (10.5)
20,001+	63 (7.5)	6 (3.7)	69 (6.9)
Total	**842 (83.8)**	**163 (16.2)**	**1005 (100.0)**

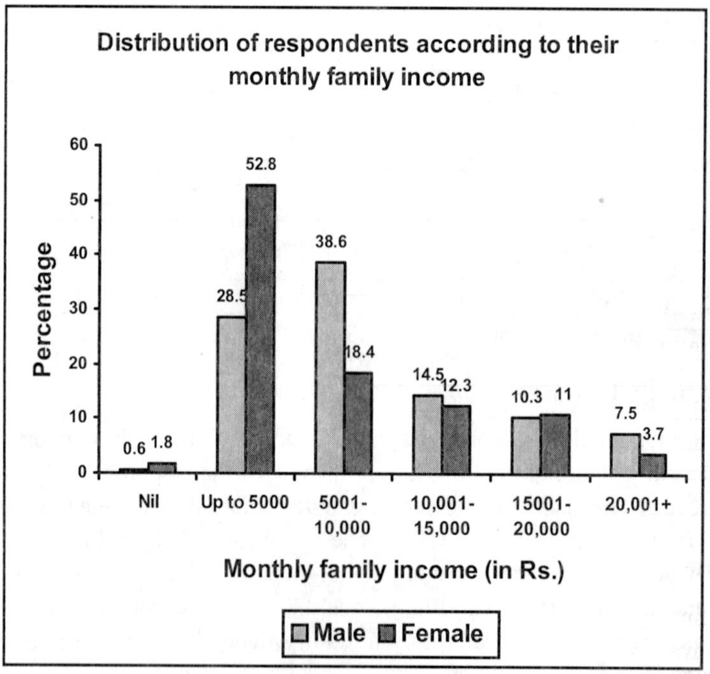

Fig. 6.2

Earners and Dependents

For proper analysis of economic status of respondent's family, it is important to know number of earners and dependants per family.

As per reported facts we can say that in a majority (51.9%) of the families have two earners, followed by those having three earners (27.1%) and those with one earner (20.2%) only. There is no earner in the remaining (0.8%) respondents' families. They are totally dependent on others.

Table 6.4: Distribution of respondents according to number of earners in their respective families

Number of earners	*Male*	*Female*	*Total*
No earners	5 (0.6)	3 (1.8)	8 (0.8)
One earner	170 (20.2)	33 (20.2)	203 (20.2)
2 earners	407 (48.3)	115 (70.6)	522 (51.9)
3+ earners	260 (30.9)	12 (7.4)	272 (27.1)
Total	**842 (83.8)**	**163 (16.2)**	**1005 (100.0)**

With regard to number of dependents members per family, it is reported that the largest segment of them (43.4%), have 4 or more dependents, followed by 32.3 percent having 2 to 3 dependents each, 19.7 percent family having one dependent each, while 0.8 percent family comprise dependent only, i.e. they have no earner.

Table 6.5: Distribution of respondents according to dependent members in the family

Number of Dependents	*Male*	*Female*	*Total*
No dependents	21 (2.5)	17 (10.4)	38 (3.8)
Only 1 dependent	180 (21.4)	18 (11.0)	198 (19.7)
2 to 3 dependents	285 (33.8)	40 (24.5)	325 (32.3)
4+ dependents	351 (41.7)	85 (52.2)	436 (43.4)
All dependents	5 (0.6)	3 (1.8)	08 (0.8)
Total	**842 (83.8)**	**163 (16.2)**	**1005 (100.0)**

Ownership of Property

Almost all the elderly reported possession of one or other form of movable or immovable property. House, land and residential plot are found to be the important forms of assets reported. Majority of the male respondents have a house (95.2%) and land or housing plot (92.6%) in their name. Sex-wise distribution clearly shows that a much larger number of men compared to women reported possession of different kinds of assets. (See table below)

Table 6.6: Distribution of respondents by possession of movable and immovable property

Type of assets	*Male N=842*	*Female N=163*	*Total N=1005*
House	802 (95.2)	28 (17.2)	830 (82.6)
Land/Plot	780 (92.6)	08 (4.9)	788 (78.4)
Livestock	387 (45.9)	05 (3.1)	392 (39.0)
Post office savings	296 (35.2)	21 (12.9)	317 (31.5)
Fixed deposits	386 (45.8)	10 (6.1)	396 (39.4)
Car/Jeep etc.	120 (14.3)	02 (1.2)	122 (12.1)
Scooter/Motor Cycle	241 (28.6)	01 (0.6)	242 (24.1)
Cycle	382 (45.4)	-	382 (38.0)
Ricksha or Sagari	25 (3.0)	03 (1.8)	25 (2.5)
Tractor/Thresher	15 (1.8)	-	15 (1.5)

* Bracket indicates percentage. Total of percentages is more than 100 due to multiple responses .

About 45 percent respondents reported that they do have income from the assets and 30 percent of the respondents said that their only source of income are assets especially land and house.

Indebtedness

As regard to debts, only 11.6 percent respondents reported having any debts. Sex-wise analysis clearly shows that 13.1 percent male and only 1.2 percent of female respondents are having debts.

Table 6.7: Distribution of respondents according to indebtedness

Debts	*Male*	*Female*	*Total*
Yes	115 (13.7)	02 (1.2)	117 (11.6)
No	727 (86.3)	161 (98.8)	888 (88.4)
Total	**842 (83.8)**	**163 (16.2)**	**1005 (100.0)**

Note: Figures in brackets indicate percentage.

The range of debt amounts shows that the largest number (51.3%) are in debted to the tune of Rs. 25000 or even less than that. 10.3 percent respondents have debts of Rs. 25001 to 50000, 12.8 percent 50001 to 75000, 8.5 percent 75001 to 100000 and remaining 17.1 percent are indebted to the extent of Rs. 100001 or more. Only two women respondents reported having any debt (Table 6.8 and Fig. 6.3). They have taken house building loan during their service period which they are still repaying after retirement. The loan amount varies between Rs. 5000/- to Rs. 15 lakh. The maximum amount of debts (15 lakh) is on account of home loan. Most of such loans are on urban respondents.

Table 6.8: Distribution of respondents by sex and by amount of debts

N=117

Loan amount (Rs.)	*Male*	*Female*	*Total*
Below 25000	60 (52.2)	-	60 (51.3)
25001-50000	12 (10.4)	-	12 (10.3)
50001-75000	15 (13.0)	-	15 (12.8)
75001-100000	10 (8.7)	-	10 (8.5)
100001+	18 (15.7)	2 (100.0)	20 (17.1)
Total	**115 (98.3)**	**02 (1.7)**	**117 (100.0)**

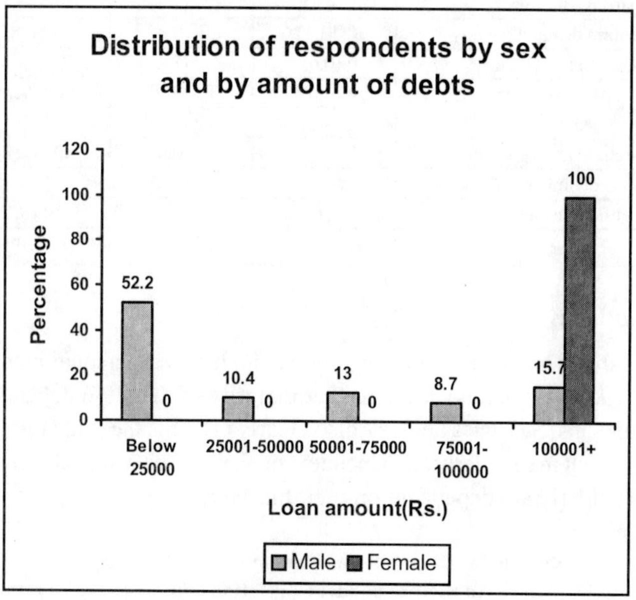

Fig. 6.3

While close to a majority (47.5%) of rural respondents has taken loan for the purposes of marriage of their daughters, a large majority (85.7%) of urban respondents have taken loans for house construction.

Among the rural respondents 16.4 percent have taken loan for agricultural purposes, 13.1 percent for rituals relating to death ceremony, 8.2 percent for medical treatment, 6.6 percent for business purposes, 4.9 percent due to economic necessity and 3.3 percent to purchase tractors.

In the urban areas as mentioned earlier the main reasons (85.7%) for debts are for house buildings, besides this the other reasons are business purposes (8.9%), medical treatment (3.6%) and for marriage purposes (1.8%).

Table 6.9: Distribution of respondents according to reasons for incurring Debt

N=117

Reasons	*Rural*	*Urban*	*Total*
For marriage purposes	29 (47.5)	1 (1.8)	30 (25.6)
To perform death ceremony	8 (13.1)	- (0.0)	8 (6.8)
For house construction	0 (0.0)	48 (85.7)	48 (41.0)
For business purposes	4 (6.6)	5 (8.9)	09 (7.7)
For treatment	5 (8.2)	2 (3.6)	07 (6.0)
To purchase tractor	2 (3.3)	- (0.0)	02 (1.7)
Due to economic problem	3 (4.9)	- (0.0)	03 (2.6)
Agricultural purposes	10 (16.4)	- (0.0)	10 (8.6)
Total	**61 (57.0)**	**56 (52.3)**	**117 (100.0)**

Dependency

As regards dependency of respondents who have no personal income (total 195 respondents), we find that majority of them are dependent on their sons. Sex-wise analysis also clearly presents the same picture. 15.4 percent male elderly are dependent on their wives, while 20 percent female elderly are dependent on their husbands.

Table 6.10: Distribution of respondents according to their dependency relationship

N= 195

Dependency on	*Male*	*Female*	*Total*
Son	45 (69.2)	93 (71.5)	138 (70.8)
Husband	- (0.0)	26 (20.0)	26 (13.4)

(Contd...)

Brother	5 (7.7)	6 (4.6)	11 (5.6)
Wife	10 (15.4)	- (0.0)	10 (5.1)
Son-in-law	3 (4.6)	5 (3.9)	8 (4.1)
Relatives	2 (3.1)	- (0.0)	2 (1.0)
Total	**65 (33.3)**	**130 (66.7)**	**195 (100.0)**

Availing Facilities for Senior Citizens

Government is providing several facilities to senior citizens. As regards availing these facilities, it was revealed that majority (73.2%) of respondents are availing them.

Table 6.11: Distribution of respondents according to availing facilities for senior citizens

Whether availing facilities?	*Frequency*	*Percentage*
Yes	736	73.2
No	269	26.8
Total	**1005**	**100.0**

Further analysis revealed that among respondents who avail facilities for senior citizens cent percent of them mainly avail concession in rail tickets. Further, 24.5 percent respondents do avail rebate in income tax, 24.3 percent enjoy the benefits of higher bank interest rates and 13.3% get Old Age Pension.

Table 6.12: Distribution of respondents according to types of facilities availed

N= 736*

Availing facilities	*Frequency*	*Percentage*
Rebate in income tax	180	24.5
Higher bank interest rate	179	24.3
Concession in rail ticket	736	100.0
Old Age Pension	98	13.3

* Multiple answers

Income Sufficiency

As regards, the respondents views on their income (N = 810, not asked from 195 respondents whose income was nil) in comparison to expenses, it was found that majority of them (63.0%) said that it is not sufficient to cover their expenses. Only 37.0 percent respondents said that their income is sufficient to cover their expenses. Most of these respondents were either class I (or equivalent) retired pensioners or big farmers or businessmen.

Table 6.13: Distribution of respondents according to income sufficiency

N=810

Response	*Frequency*	*Percentage*
Sufficient to cover expenses	300	37.0
Not sufficient	510	63.0
Total	**810**	**100.0**

In cases of income deficit it would be interesting to know how they manage to meet their expenses. It was found that majority of them (95.7 percent) either cut down their expenses (49.0%), or take the help of their sons or daughters (46.7%) or take short term loan from relatives or friends (4.3%).

Table 6.14: Distribution of respondents according to their ways to balance income and expenditure

N=510

Ways to manage	*Frequency*	*Percentage*
By cutting down expenses	250	49.0
Take help from sons/ daughter etc.	238	46.7
By taking short term loans	22	4.3
Total	**510**	**100.0**

Attempt to Grab their Property

It is generally found that property is one of the main issue over which conflict arose between the elderly and the abuser. But as can be seen from the table below, this issue is not much prevalent among our respondents. Only 9.7 percent respondents (majority of them, 84.5% are male) have said that they had to encounter any threat of dispossession from their property by any of their family members.

Table 6.15: Distribution of respondents according to family member's attempt to grab their property

Response	*Male*	*Female*	*Frequency*
Yes	82 (84.5%)	15 (15.5%)	97 (9.7%)
No	760 (83.7%)	148 (16.3%)	908 (90.3%)
Total	**842 (83.8%)**	**163 (16.2%)**	**1005 (100.0%)**

We have further explored from the 97 respondents that what were the different forms of abuse perpetrated against them by those trying to grab the property. We have received multiple responses; it means the respondent experienced multiple forms of abuses- verbal, psychological, and physical (Table 6.16 and Fig. 6.4).

Table 6.16: Distribution of respondents according to type of abuse perpetrated on them

N= 97*

Verbal abuse and/or neglect	100.0
Threatening	89.0
Physical abuse	8.0
Psychological/emotional pressure	85.0

* Multiple responses.

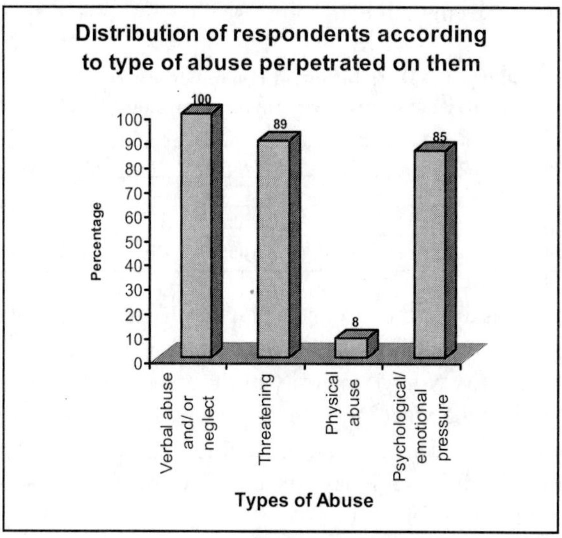

Fig. 6.4

It is obvious from the above table that cent percent respondents experienced verbal abuse or/and neglect. Threatening (89%) psychological/ emotional pressures (85.0 %), and physical abuse (8%) are the other forms of abuse used with the intention to grab elderly persons' property.

To explore possibilities of financial and material abuse, we asked our respondents whether they have ever signed a document which they could not understand. Only 4 respondents said 'yes' they had signed such a document. It is quite obvious that they were victims of financial abuse.

Table 6.17: Distribution of respondents according to signing of document which they could not understand

Signed	*Frequency*	*Percentage*
Yes	04	0.4
No	1001	99.6
Total	**1005**	**100.0**

Property distribution and feeling of neglect

It is revealed that almost half of the respondents (47.8%) have already distributed their property (movable or immovable) among their sons and in a few cases to their daughters also.

Table 6.18: Distribution of respondents according to division of property among sons/daughters

Response	*Frequency*	*Percentage*
Yes	480	47.8
No	525	52.2
Total	**1005**	**100.0**

When we asked to the respondents if they had experienced neglect by their son/sons after they were given a share in the property? It was surprising that a very large majority of the respondents (89.2%) said 'Yes', they are experiencing neglect by them. Normally, one would have expected that such act of unselfishness on the part of elderly will have a positive effect, but it have the contrary effect; the beneficiaries proved themselves selfish.

Table 6.19: Distribution of respondents according to their feelings of neglect after property distribution

N=480

Feeling	*Frequency*	*Percentage*
Neglected	428	89.2
Not neglected	52	10.8
Total	**480**	**100.0**

Litigation on Landed Property

Litigation and that too, on landed property, is very common in rural India. Keeping this in view, we have tried to find out from our respondents that whether any property litigation is going on with own family members or relatives (See tables below).

Table 6.20: Distribution of respondents according to property litigation with family members

N = 830

Litigation	*Frequency*	*Percent*
Yes	56	6.7
No	774	93.3
Total	**830**	**100.0**

Table 6.21: Distribution of respondents according to ongoing litigations

N=56

Litigations	*Frequency*	*Percentage*
Yes, going on	12	21.4
No	44	78.6
Total	**56**	**100.0**

It was found that majority (93.3%) of the respondents are involved in no litigation at all. Only a few (6.7%) respondents had faced any litigation, but among them (among 6.7 %) 21.4 percent are facing it currently.

Chapter - 7

Elder Abuse: Forms and Pattern

In India the issue of elder abuse and neglect can no longer be ignored (Shankardass, Mala Kapur, 2010: 189). Elder abuse exists, though it may not be widely acknowledged. Today, the problem of elder abuse affects a large number of senior citizens in the society. A few Indian studies which has been already mentioned earlier in the survey of literature, also gave strong indications as to the existence of maltreatment of senior citizens in the family context. The maltreatment of the elderly significantly undermines the quality of their life and may have a profound effect on the moral fiber of the majority. (B. Devi Prasad, 2008: 2).

There are no reliable national level data in India on the prevalence and incidence of elder abuse and neglect. In this study we have tried to know about the occurrence of abuse among our respondents (See table below)

Table 7.1: Distribution of respondents by occurrence of abuse

Occurrence	*Men*	*Women*	*Total*
Abused	168 (20.0)	70 (43.0)	238 (23.7)
Not abused	674 (80.0)	93 (57.0)	767 (76.3)
Total	**842 (83.8)**	**163 (16.2)**	**1005 (100.0)**

Note: Figures in the brackets indicates percentage.

It is obvious from the above table that elder abuse does exist in our society as a significant i.e. 23.7 percent of the respondents have said that they were being abused. Gender-wise analysis clearly shows that female respondents were more abused than their male counterparts.

We have also analyzed the incidence of abuse by marital status. It was found that slightly higher percentage of widowed, separated and unmarried fell in the abused category as compared to the non-abused. Among married a higher percentage (82.4%) was in the not abused group (See Table 7.2 and Fig. 7.1).

Table 7.2: Distribution of respondents by marital status and by occurrence of abuse

Marital status	*Abused*	*Non-abused*	*Total*
Married	128 (17.6)	599 (82.4)	727 (72.3)
Unmarried	1 (33.4)	2 (66.6)	3 (0.3)
Widowed	105 (38.7)	166 (61.3)	271 (27.0)
Separated	4 (100.0)	0 (0.0)	4 (0.4)
Total	**238 (23.7)**	**767 (76.3)**	**1005 (100.0)**

Note: Figures in brackets are percentage.

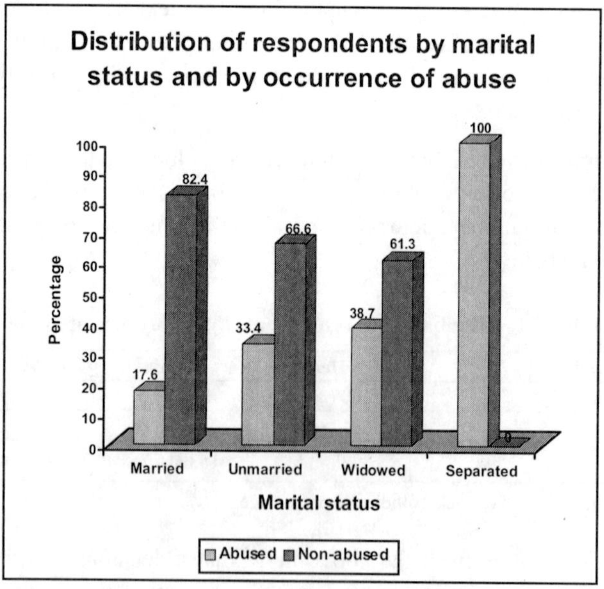

Fig. 7.1

It was realized that it was very difficult to answer what factors place the elderly at risk. On the basis of primary data collected through interview-schedule and facts collected through FGDs, we found that it is a multidimensional phenomenon resulting from the interaction of several factors. We may mention a few potential risk factors as-*

1. Individual level factors of the elderly such as poor physical health status (especially functional impairment or dementia), and other abnormal personality characteristics, alcoholic or other bad habits.
2. Social isolation- fewer contacts with neighbours, friends and relatives.
3. Power and exchange dynamics in the relationship such as abuser dependency, and victim's dependency leading to caregiver stress.
4. Individual level factors of the abuser such as longstanding personality traits (like bad temper, hypercritical etc.) Or alcoholic or drug abuser or dependency.
5. Dominating and aggressive nature of both- victim and abuser.

It is important to know about the chief abuser. Several studies have revealed the relationship of victim to perpetrator. It may be adult son (Veedon, 2001; Vijayalakshmi, 2001; Yan and Tang, 2004; Chokkanathan and Lee, 2005; Patel, 2005; NCEA, 2006) or spouses (Pillemer and Finkelhor, 1998) or sons and daughter-in-law (Rao, 1995, Srinivas, 1996, Vijaykumar, 1999, Oh. J. et.al, 2006; Devi Prasad, 2008; Avataramu, 2008).

We have requested our respondents to disclose their relationship with chief abuser. As can be seen, son (45.4%) and daughter-in-law (26.5%) figured as the most frequently mentioned actors in the perpetration of abuse against the elderly. The next in that order are brother's wife (6.3%) and in the case of female respondent their Jethani/Devrani i.e. husband's elder/younger brother's wife (5.0%) (Table 7.3 and Fig. 7.2).

---

* British Geriatric Society (2003) and Bonnie and Wallace (2002) has identified some of the above potential risk factors in their studies which was presented by Devi Prasad (2008:9) in his work.

Table 7.3: Distribution of respondents by their relationship with chief abusers

N=238

Relationship	*Respondents*	
	Male	*Female*
Son	102 (60.7)	6 (8.6)
Daughter-in-law	34 (20.2)	29 (41.4)
Wife	9 (5.4)	-
Husband	-	10 (14.3)
Brother	6 (3.6)	2 (2.9)
Husband's brother	-	6 (8.6)
Jethani/Devrani	-	12 (17.1)
Grand son	6 (3.6)	-
Daughter	-	1 (1.4)
Brother's wife	11 (6.5)	4 (5.7)
Total	**168 (70.6)**	**70 (29.4)**

Note: figures in brackets are percentage.

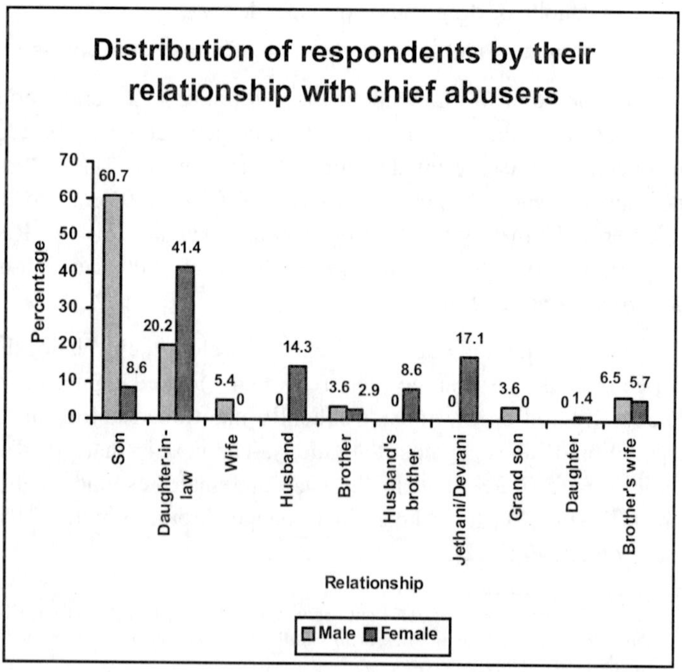

Fig. 7.2

If we take male respondents separately, next to son (60.7%), the daughter- in -law (20.2%) figured as the hardest person to get along with. 5.4 percent respondents have mentioned their wife as chief abuser. On the other side when we take female respondents separately, next to daughter-in-law (41.4%) Jethani/Devrani (17.1%) and husband (14.3%) figured as chief abusers. Of the 238 respondents who reported abuse; majority (45.4 %) was abused by their sons followed by daughter-in-law (26.5%). A significant proportion of spouse abuse was also found (by wife 5.4% and by husband 14.3%).

We have tried to explore reasons for elder abuse. For this an attempt has been made to identity the issues over which conflict arose. The issues were different among male and female elderly. If we take only male elderly, the disagreement appeared to centre mostly on issues as demand of money or property (23.8%), demand for special care at the time of illness or due to ill health (20.2%), lack of privacy and freedom (15.6%) and demanding nature of elderly (13.1%).

Table 7.4: Distribution of respondents according to issues over which abuse starts

N= 238*

Issues of conflict	*Men (N=168)*	*Women (N=70)*
Demand of money/property by abuser	40 (23.8)	9 (12.9)
Special care at the time of or due to ill health	34 (20.2)	15 (21.4)
Issue of providing food	8 (4.8)	8 (11.4)
Insisting on the elderly to live separately	15 (8.9)	5 (7.1)
Due to habits of elderly (Alcohol use/ Smoking/early rising etc.)	19 (11.3)	2 (2.9)
Conflict due to child rearing issues	2 (1.2)	15 (21.4)
Demanding nature of elderly	22 (13.1)	3 (4.3)
Conflict on the issue of household chores	16 (9.5)	40 (57.1)
Forcing elderly to work	10 (6.0)	6 (8.6)
Express unwillingness to take care of elderly	20 (11.9)	4 (5.7)
Issue of privacy and freedom	26 (15.6)	12 (17.1)
Due to expenses on treatment	30 (17.9)	15 (21.4)

* Total of percentage is more than 100 as several respondents have mentioned more than one issue.

It is obvious from the table that more women (57.1%) reported household chores as the main issue of conflict or arguments. The other issues are ill health or special care at the time of ill health (21.4%), expenses on treatment (21.4%), child rearing matters (21.4%) etc.

Patterns of abuse

We know about the different forms of abuse. Several western scholars like Lau and Kosberg, 1979; Pillemer and Finkelhor,1988 have found physical violence as the most widespread form of abuse, whereas others like Block and Sinnott, 1979, Steur and Austine, 1980; Wolf and others,1986 have found psychological abuse and financial abuse and neglect as the most prevalent forms of abuse.

Indian scholars like Rao, 1995; Srinivas, 2004; Sivaraju, 2003, Devi Prasad, 2008; Avataramu, 2008 have not found in their studies physical abuse as most prevalent pattern of elder abuse.

Since 23.7 percent of the respondents have disclosed that they were experiencing abuse, it is important to know what are the different forms of abuse perpetrated against them. What pattern of elder abuse emerges from our respondents' may be seen from the following table.

Table No.7.5: Distribution of respondents according to nature of abuse experienced

N=238*

Nature of Abuse	*Male N=168*	*Female N=70*
Verbal abuse	168 (100.0)	70 (100.0)
Physical abuse	10 (5.9)	12 (17.1)
Socio-psychological abuse	168 (100.0)	70 (100.0)
Economic abuse	105 (62.5)	18 (25.7)
Neglect	168 (100.0)	70 (100.0)

* The total of percentage is more than 100 as some of the respondents have mentioned more than one form of abuse.

It is obvious from the above table that among (23.7%) the abused males and females, cent percent respondents (100.0%) reported having experiencing socio-psychological abuse and repeated incidences of verbal abuse and neglect. 62.5 percent male respondents and

25.7 percent female respondents have reported facing economic abuse. Among respondents not an insignificant percentage reported experiencing the worst kind of abuse that is physical abuse, 17.1 percent female and 5.9 percent male respondents have reported experiencing physical abuse.

In terms of the forms of abuse used by different abusers an important insights has emerged from the study that while physical and economic abuse is generally inflicted by sons, verbal and psychological abuse is perpetrated by daughters-in-law and that too in some cases together with their mothers-in-law. Further, useful insights have emerged from the study through in-depth interviews that economic abuse was jointly done by wife and son and in some cases with daughter-in-law, wherein all of them jointly pressurized the elderly male to handover large sum of money to son for starting business or other work. Not a single case has been found where daughter put pressure on her parents to transfer money or valuables or property to her.

As part of pattern of abuse several forms of abusive behavior by the abuser have been revealed. For instance, it was revealed by the respondents who have reported experiencing verbal abuse, that cent percent of them have to put up with scolding, rude or aggressive behavior of the abuser.

Physically abused respondents have to face slapping, pushing/ shaking and physical injury by the abusers. Neglect, insult, humiliation/ harassment are some of the forms of socio-psychological abuse which have to be faced by cent percent respondents. Cheating and stealing of money are the main forms of economic abuse which have to be faced by almost cent percent respondents.

Table 7.6: Distribution of respondents according to facing different forms of abuse

Pattern and Forms	*Male*	*Female*
Verbal abuse (Male=168, Female=70):-		
- abusive language	38.0	52.0
- scolding	100.0	100.0
- rude/aggressive responses	100.0	100.0

(Contd...)

Physical abuse (Male=10, Female=12)		
- kicking	20.0	25.0
- slapping	40.0	16.6
- pushing/shaking	40.0	58.3
- pinching	30.0	50.0
- beating/hitting by object	40.0	33.3
- locked in room/tied to bed	20.0	16.6
Socio-psychological (Male=168, Female=70)		
- neglect	100.0	100.0
- insult	100.0	100.0
- threat	65.4	57.1
- humiliation/harassment	100.0	100.0
- social isolation	14.2	25.7
- threats to put in old age home	10.7	28.5
- refused to talk	24.4	45.7
Economic abuse (Male=105, Female=18)		
- cheating/stealing money	100.0	100.0
- grabbing property	78.0	83.3
- pressurizing to work/earn money	23.0	44.4

Frequency of incidence of different items of abuse

It is important to analyze item wise frequency of the occurrence of the abuse suffered by the elderly during the last five years. It was revealed that cent percent respondents reported occurrence of verbal abuse (especially scolding and rude/ aggressive behaviour), socio-psychological abuse (like insult, humiliation / harassment and neglect) and economic abuse (like cheating or stealing money) almost daily since last five years.

5.9 percent male and 17.1 percent female respondents who have reported that they were subjected to physical abuse have mentioned various forms of physical abuse such as kicking, slapping, pushing/ shaking, pinching, beating up/ hitting by object, locked in a room, and tied to bed. Further, it is revealed that frequency of slapping and incidence of beating up were very less in comparison to other forms of physical abuse.

We have also tried to find out the relationship between gender and incidence of violence and marital status and incidence of violence and age and incidence of violence. As regards to gender and incidence of violence it was found that pushing, shaking and pinching are the prevalent forms of abuse to female elderly, while male elderly suffer from beating up, hitting or slapping. The marital status wise incidence of violence clearly shows that except in the cases of a few widows, there is no relation between incidence of violence and marital status. Likewise, age and incidence of violence has also not very significant relation exist. Violence is generally issue based, it is not very much connected with other variables like age and marital status or gender. The sick and frail elderly are more vulnerable than others.

Giving Information of Mistreatment

We have tried to know from our 238 identified respondents who have been the victims of elder abuse at one time or other, about giving information to their near or dear ones at the time of abuse. It was found that majority (72.7%) of them have not given information to anybody about their mistreatment, while 19.7 percent of them have given information to other family members, 3.4 % to their neighbors and 4.2 % to relatives. It means that the older persons prefer to silently suffer abuse, than tell others about it.

Table 7.7: Distribution of abused respondents according to giving information of mistreatment

N=238

Information given to	*Frequency*	*Percentage*
Relatives	10	4.2
Neighbours	8	3.4
Other family members	47	19.7
None	173	72.7
Total	**238**	**100.0**

We have asked from our those respondents (total 173 in number) who have reported that they have not given information of mistreatment to anybody the reason for not seeking help during conflict situations. Majority (55.6%) of the male respondents have said that they did not want to disgrace family by seeking help from others. While majority (46.1%) of the female have not informed others in apprehension that they might be subjected to further abuse. Almost equal number (43.1%)

of female elderly said that it is of no use as it is part of life, no body will come to help.

Table 7.8: Distribution of elderly by their reasons for not seeking help during conflict situations

N=173

Reasons	Male	Female	Total
Didn't want to disgrace family	60 (55.6%)	5 (7.7%)	65 (37.6%)
It is of no use	10 (9.3%)	28 (43.1%)	38 (22.0%)
Felt embarrassed to ask for help	25 (23.1%)	2 (3.1%)	27 (15.6%)
Afraid of further abuse	13 (12.0%)	30 (46.1%)	43 (24.8%)
Total	**108 (62.4%)**	**65 (37.6%)**	**173 (100.0%)**

It is fact that elder abuse often goes unreported on account of several factors. Lowenstein, Doron & Winterstein (2004) has mentioned them as-

- It being a family affair,
- Hesitation to label a child or spouse as an abuser,
- Embarrassment,
- Fear of being labelled demented or in capable,
- Fear of retaliation,
- Fear of being removed from home is worse than the abuse,
- Lack of social and familial awareness,
- Isolation of some groups of older persons, especially migrants,
- Lack of awareness concerning whom to report,
- Belief among the elders that they are the cause of the problem, and
- Belief among the elders that they are being paid back for their earlier abuse of spouse or child.

Awareness of National Policy

Govt. of India enacted the National Policy on Older Persons in 1999. Since then several programes and schemes have been launched for the welfare of the older persons. With regard to awareness of this National Policy, we have come to know that an overwhelming majority (96.4%) of the respondents were not aware of this policy.

Table 7.9: Distribution of respondents according to awareness of National Policy for Older Persons

Response	*Frequency*	*Percentage*
Yes	36	3.6
No	969	96.4
Total	1005	100.0

Such low level of awareness of the policy and programmes intended for their benefit, given the sizable urban and literate, educated in fact, is rather amazing.

Suggestions to Stop Elder Abuse

Though our respondents are not aware that the National Policy on Older Persons and its provisions, they readily give their suggestions with regard to governmental efforts to stop elder abuse. Majority of the respondents (92.0%) have said that government's economic support is essential to stop elder abuse. 94.5 percent respondents have said that government should provide free medical facilities to elderly persons, while 69.4 percent respondents said that special care provision should be made by the government, 26.8 percent respondents have said that special laws should be enacted by the government to stop elder abuse, while 19.5 percent respondents said that special incentives be given to care givers to stop elder abuse. To conclude, we may say that majority of the respondents feel that economic and health related support measures are essential to stop the elder abuse.

Table 7.10: Distribution of respondents according to their suggestions for governmental efforts to stop elder abuse*

Suggestions	*Percentage*
Economic support	92.0
Free medical facilities	94.5
Special care provisions	69.4
Special laws to stop abuse	26.8
Special incentives to care givers	19.5

* Multiple responses

Legal Recourse under 2007 Act

Government of India enacted a special law, Maintenance and Welfare of Parents and Senior Citizens Act, 2007 to stop elder abuse and protect elderly person from abuse. The Salient Features of the Act ensure maintenance of Parents and Senior Citizens within their family, places a legal obligation on children and relatives to maintain their parents; prescribes setting up of Tribunals for quick settlement of maintenance claims, avoids Cumbersome Legal Procedure and recommends setting up Old Age Homes in all Districts.

We have tried to know from our respondents whether any protection was sought by them under this act. The information received is presented below in the table 7.11.

Table 7.11: Distribution of respondents according to legal recourse under 2007 Act

Help taken	*Frequency*	*Percentage*
Yes	01	0.1
No	1004	99.9
Total	**1005**	**100.0**

It is obvious from the above table that only one respondent has lodged complaint under this act.

Chapter - 8

Case Studies of Victims of Elder Abuse And Neglect

Case Study: 1

85 years old Mr. A retired from central university. He was IVth class employee for about 40 years. Originally he belonged to Deoria and after retirement finally settled at Varanasi. His wife expired in year 2000. By his family background, he was economically very poor and at his native place he possess one bigha land only. He has two sons, elder one studied up to high school and after that joined service in the postal department as a post man at Deoria and the younger one did PhD in Sociology from a central university. Mr. A spent his meager hard earned money on the education of his younger son. He tried his best to provide all the facilities and comforts to him. On his demand he has even purchased a motor cycle for him. After completion of PhD degree, his son joined service in an ICMR project and later on married.

Mr. A had spent a large amount of money on his son and was expecting some money from him after he joined service. But his son was not willing to give a single penny to him. One day when he came on leave, Mr. A asked him about his salary and demanded some money. His son became very angry and refused to disclose anything about his salary. Mr. A was shocked to see his behaviour. Since that day the daughter-in-law's behaviour also changed and she has started neglecting him. Mr. A was psychologically very upset with this type of abuse and neglect. He also stopped talking with them.

After few years his son went abroad and joined service in a project. He was getting good salary over there. His wife and sons stayed back with Mr.A. From abroad his son has been sending money to his wife. After knowing this, Mr. A told his daughter-in-law to give some money for repairing the house and for other necessities. The daughter-in-law refused to give any money and also she informed her husband about his demand. Mr. A became mentally upset when his son abused him on phone from abroad. When his son returned on vacation, an altercation took ugly turns and Mr. A was beaten his son. Mr. A decided not to take any help from them in future and started working by himself despite of his old age of 85 years.

Sometimes when he finds it difficult to cook, he eats in a neighbor's house. One day when he was asking a glass of milk from his neighbour, the neighbour told him to get it from his own daughter-in-law. Mr. A started criticizing his daughter-in-law's behaviour. On hearing such criticism Mr. A's son and daughter-in-law physically abused him. They were stopped by the intervention of neighbours.

The neighbors informed the local media about this case of elder abuse and neglect. One day media visited and tried to make a story of such inhuman treatment and violation of human rights. It was shown by a national channel too.

(Mr. A died during the study period.)

Case Study: 2

80 years old Mrs. B is a Bengali widow. Her husband was a bank manager and died 15 year ago. Mrs. B has two sons elder one is a manager in a bank and younger one is mentally disabled. She was living with her sons in a good house which was in her name. Elder son's family was also staying in that house. One day her elder son requested her to transfer her house in his name so that he could get bank-loan for its renovation. Mrs. B honoured the request of his son. The house was transferred to the name of her elder son.

After getting the house transferred in his name, one day Mrs. B's elder son informed him that he has received transfer orders and he has to join there soon. He requested his mother to accompany him alone and leave his mentally disabled brother somewhere at Varanasi.

Mrs. B was shocked to hear this. She requested him several times to change his attitude and accept him as both of them were her sons and equally dear to her. But her elder son refused to accept her request and left the house and proceeded the place of his new posting with his family. After one year, without her knowledge and consent he sold the house and gradually the new owner forced Mrs. B to vacate the house and took possession of it.

There was no option left for Mrs. B. She tried to contact her son but she could not contact him as his phone number had changed. She was taken shelter in a gumti near her house with her mentally disabled son. At the time of interview she was getting a family pension which was the source of livelihood.

(Mrs. B died during the research period.)

Case Study: 3

Mrs. C is a 80 years old illiterate widow. Her husband died when she was 50 years old. She has two sons and two daughters. Her younger son and daughter-in-law committed suicide 15 years back. Her only elder son is an alcoholic, who works in a bead manufacturing unit at Varanasi. Whatever land was there in the name of Mrs. C, it was sold by her son.

Few years back he left his ancestral house along with his family. When Mrs. C enquired about the reason for leaving the house, he told her that it would be convenient for him to live near his work place. Mrs. C was left alone in her house. Later on, one day a man came and asked her to vacate the house as he has purchased it from his son. Mrs. C was stunned to know this. On the intervention of neighbours she was allowed to stay there till she made alternate arrangements. Mrs. C stayed there for few months and thereafter shifted to a rented house nearby. Currently she is staying with her grandson's family and sells fruits from a very small shop.

Case Study: 4

70 years old Mr. D retired as a professor from a central university. He has two sons and two daughters. All sons and daughters are married. His wife expired 8 years ago. He lives with his younger son and his

family. His elder son is government doctor, and lives separately in the city.

According to Mr. D, he has given good education to the elder son and spent a huge sum on his education. His doctor son was also good to him for the last several years, but suddenly after the marriage of his younger son, started quarreling with him.

Since the elder son is a qualified doctor and earning good money, he thought that it was his responsibility to make younger son's family financially stable. The day he discussed about his decisions to transfer the house in the name of his younger daughter-in-law, the elder son started quarreling with Mr. D and demanded an equal share. Keeping in view of his younger son's mental disabilities, Mr. D transferred his house in the name of younger son's wife i.e. his daughter –in-law so that after his death they will not have to face any housing and financial problems.

One day, when the elder son came to know that the house has been transfer in the name of his younger brother's wife, he physically abused his father and charged that he has illicit relations with the daughter- in- law. Since then, the elder son has visited his father's house several times and, threatened him to give 25 lakhs as early as possible, otherwise he will kill him. Mr. D tried to convince him, but he was not ready to listen. Other family members and relatives tried to persuade him (elder son) but he was not listening to anyone. Some of the relatives also took his side and instigated him against Mr. D. Due to such family tension Mr. D realized that his academic work and commitment are suffering badly. Therefore he refused accepting any extra remunerative assignments to be completed beyond office hours.

One day when his elder son physically assaulted him, he reported the matter to the local police station. Police visited his elder son's house and warned him of police action. On the intervention of the police Mr. D has got some relief from this problem.

(Mr. D expired during research period. His eldest son was not informed about his death. The last rites were done in the absence of the elder son, a serious departure from the traditional practice.)

Case Study: 5

70 years old Mr. E is a big businessman and he lives in the heart of the Varanasi city in a joint family. He has two daughters and three sons, all married.

Mr. E said that he was very happy and satisfied with his life as there was no Socio-Economic problem in the family since beginning. All the three son's alongwith their families were staying with Mr. E. All the members have very cordial relations with each other. According to Mr. E the problem started since last two years after his wife expired. He feels very lonely and sad when he return from his business alongwith his son, he finds there is nobody in the house to welcome him and chat him with love and affection. Sons are welcomed by their respective wives and they go inside their rooms. Very often the sons go for outing with their families and they even go to distant places on vacations. They have their own world and he himself feels lonely. Mr. E said that it is very difficult for him to pass time at home though all the facilities are there. He find himself neglected by family members.

During long interactions, it was realized that he was under going severe psychological strain and he needed proper attention by the family members and also counseling by a psychologist.

(It is unfortunate that Mr. E committed suicide recently.)

Case Study: 6

90 Years old Mrs. F is a widow. She lives in her own house with one of her son's family. She has three daughters and four sons. All of there are married and working. She recalled her earlier days when her husband was alive. According to her, there was absolutely no problem during those days. All the sons were well settled by that time and relations with them was very cordial and warm.

Since the family was too large and there were several other responsibilities, her husband could not construct house earlier. According to Mrs. E her husband did job for about 30 years and saved money to construct a good house in a good locality after her retirement. But after her death all the sons started claiming their share of the property. Mrs. E opposed this. Dispute about the father's property among the sons led to the mother's maltreatment. The son with whom Mrs. E was staying claimed a larger share of the property as he was taking care of the mother. Since Mrs. E was a family pensioner, all the brothers were expecting a share from that money also. The son with whom Mrs. E was staying was claiming his right over her pension money but Mrs. E refused to give the total pension amount to him. Whenever Mrs. E gives some money to one or other son or his children, the other ones are much displeased with her, especially the son and daughter in law with whom she was staying. Slowly an argument started between them which took an ugly turn and son and daughter-in-law started causing verbal abuse and sometimes physical abuse too, to the old lady. The relations between brothers also became tense.

Mrs. E was very upset with the abusive behaviour of the sons and daughter-in-law with whom she was staying. Later on, no son was ready to take care of her. For some time she stayed with another son's family, since both the spouses were working, it was difficult for them to take proper care of their mother. Mrs. E also realized this and returned after a few months.

All the brothers were interested to sell out the residential property and have equal distribution of the amount. The son with whom Mrs. E was residing claimed a larger share of it for the reason that not only he is looking after the elderly mother but he was spending money on the maintenance of the house. The other brothers did not agree to his claim and the dispute continued. It was the mother, who had to bear the burnt of it.

Mrs. E told me that she was abused by her son and daughter-in-law several times; all types of abuses i.e. physical, psychological, economic and also neglect were being heaped upon her.

Case Study: 7

Mr. G is 72 years old. His wife deceased 4 years back. He has three sons and two daughters. The first and second sons are in jobs and living away from the native place and third son is living with his father. He has his wife and two sons. The third son is a shopkeeper and earns a meager income to support the family. Two daughters of the case are married and living away in distant places. The case was a petty businessman himself but has no wealth. The case is totally dependent upon his third son and his wife.

The case is physically frail and has to incur a substantial amount of money on his treatment. Sometimes the first son and the second son provide some money for the treatment of father but the larger burden of care and treatment fells upon the third son, who finds it difficult to provide satisfactory treatment to the father. The wife of the third son is very irritant because she is worried all the time about education and future of her kids. For her the old man is a burden and the meager financial income of her husband is insufficient for the adequate care of the old man as well as future development of her own kids. The situation has led to neglect of the older one, neither the food nor medical care is satisfactorily available to the older one. Sometimes the older one asks for nutritious food and good medical treatment. In the absence of these, the older one has become very depressed. He always wishes death to come and save him from the miseries of life. Whenever the married daughters come to meet him he feels relatively happy but then he also feels depressed because he could not give any gift or valuables to his daughter on her visit. Life has become a long battle filled with depression, solitude and helplessness.

Case Study: 8

Mrs. H is a widower. Her husband died 15 years back. She is living with her elder son and his wife. Being the wife of a businessman, she had a comfortable life during her husband's time but after his death the situation changed. The other two sons are living separately and keep no relationship with the parental family because of property dispute among the brothers. They claim that they had been denied the share in the parental property. One daughter of the case is married and she too keeps no relationships from the parental family as her husband's family complain that no proper dowry was given at the time of marriage.

The case has developed a very pitiable life because neither the other two sons nor the daughter maintain any relationship with her. Moreover, the wife of the eldest son with whom she is living has very troublesome relationship with her. Their temperament does not match with each other. The daughter-in-law thinks that the old lady is very irritating and never happy with whatever food and care she provides to her. The old lady complains that the food she gets is not sufficient, she wants milk daily which is not provided to her. Whenever the older lady complains, she is rebutted by the daughter-in-law. Sometimes this results into use of abusive language by the daughter-in-law. She is denied food for number of days. When she draws attention of her close relatives and neighbors, she is further abused and physically assaulted by the daughter-in-law. The life of old lady is becoming miserable day by day. She has no one to look to who would listen to her grievances and provide some help.

Case Study: 9

Mr. I is 67 years old. He had one son who died long back. He then adopted the son of his sister, provided him education and when the adopted son became young he got him married. At present the old man is living with the adopted son's family. For sometime now, the old man and adopted son are estranged. The wife of the adopted son insists that the property of the old man should be transferred to their name. The old man does not want this to be done immediately. He suspects if it happens, then the chances are that he would be neglected and might even be thrown out of the house. The adopted son's wife is becoming increasingly aggressive. She always passes sarcastic remarks against the old man. She often comments that the old man has always taken benefit of the adopted son's care and protection, but now he is not transferring the property to him. The old man on his part thinks that the wife of the adopted son always thinks of the property and does not provide adequate care and comfort to him. The old man often threatens that he will give the property in charity to some welfare organization. Thus, there is always altercation in the family and the old man one has become psychological wreck.

Case Study: 10

Mrs. J is 60 years old. She is a widow, her husband died 20 years ago. Her two sons also died quite early in life. At present, she is living with her only daughter and her husband in the in her own house in which she had lived. The house is old but quite big. At present the old lady is facing quite a complicated problem because of the family property.

Some of the neighboring goondas are pressurizing the old lady to dispose of the property in their favour. The husband of her daughter is a weak person both physically and financially. He feels it would be better to dispose of the property, because he cannot deal with the goondas. Moreover, he needs money to start some new business and to live in some other place where the goonda may not threaten him. The old lady is quite perturbed. She is very much attached to the family property. She wants to die in the family home. She has reported the matter to the police authority but the goondas have bribed the police and no positive action was initiated to protect her from the goons and to protect the property. The daughter has become furious. She thinks that the mother is a quarrelsome person and proving to be a hurdle in disposing of the family property. She has become very irritant and uses abusive languages against her mother. She denied food to her one time every day. There is altercation in the home almost daily. The old lady is very much disturbed because her own daughter is not giving the due respect and care which she deserves.

Case Study: 11

Mr. K is 70 years old. He lives in slum area of the city in a small house with three of his sons who are married, have wives and children. Life is miserable in the small house with no proper ventilation and sanitation facility. The case lost his wife fifteen years back and his sons and their wives take care of him. The case has got no income of his own. The income of the sons who have petty shops or menial jobs is not sufficient to run the family comfortably. Its hard life so far as the education of the children and fulfillment of bare necessities of life is concerned. The old man is suffering from bronchitis. He needs proper and regular medicine. The family finds difficult to provide adequate medical care. The old man rebukes his sons for not providing him proper medical care. The sons always say that they hardly manage to provide a little food for the family. There is not enough money to provide better medical and health care to the old man. The result is that the old man feels distance alienated from his progeny and distrusts them. Poverty of the family has caused neglect of the old man by the younger generation. The human warmth and the proverbial respect for the old in the family is missing.

Case Study: 12

Mr. L is 72 years old. He has three sons and one daughter. All of them are married and living separately away from the home. The old man lives with her wife who is almost crippled. He has taken the aid of a male domestic servant who cooks food and does all the necessary work outside the house. The old man spends his time in reading newspaper or watching TV. He regularly goes for morning walk and spends some time in gossiping with the older people. Back home he has no problem as his wife is helpless and quite submissive. The domestic servant is quite obedient. He has enough bank account to manage the family budget. In spite of all this the old man is quite lonely and is gradually developing a feeling of despondency towards life. He always thinks that having sons and daughter have no meaning, if they cannot give him company and comfort in old age. Sometimes they visit the parents but they have their own family life and an obligation to fulfill. The old man is gradually becoming withdrawn and reticent. He feels that the old age needs the company of the family, more than the financial stability.

Case Study: 13

Mr. 'X' is a retired Professor of a central university and lives in his own house. He has two sons and one daughter. His daughter is married and lives at Delhi with her family. Elder son is also married and employed. He too lives at Delhi with his family. The younger sons who is a divorce lives with him.

During the field work the researcher came to know that Mr. 'X' is very sad and depressed due to his sons habits. After repeated request to Mr 'X' he agreed to give indepth interview.

Mr 'X' told me that his life was very smooth for several decades. There was no problem in the family. His family was small and all family members were very cordial to each other. The problem started few years back when his younger son went for marriage with another professors daughter.

The daughter-in-law was very good. His younger son was very ambitious but would not get good job. After marriage he become contractor and later on purchased one JCB Machine. In the beginning everything was alight but gradually his son started drinking outside with fellow contractors and friends. His wife did not like it, and quarrel started between them soon. But when his son has not changed his habits, his wife left the house with her daughter. She was working in a school and was very nice to them.

Mr. X's son became habitual drunker since the day his wife and family left the house. He was not able to do his work. He has incurred heavy loss in business, so he could not repay the loan amount to Bank. Mr. 'X' paid a few installments but he was also not in a position to pay heavy installments. The vehicle was seized by the Bank. Often, his son came home drunk and demanded money and if they did not give, he would yell at him and sometimes at his mother and also resorted to physical abuse. Seeing his sons habits, marital and socio-economic condition Mr. 'X' wife was very much disturbed and shocked. Due to this she died last year. Mr. 'X' is completely disturbed after his wife's death but his son has not changed his habits. Mr. X's problems are increasing day by day as his sons habits are becoming worse. He has started stealing in the house and selling household goods. He don't know how to stop all this.

(Note: Recently Mr. X's younger son died due to heavy drinking. Mr. 'X' is now alone in the house and there is nobody to look after him. When I met after his son's death he broke down and asked how to live alone, could you please bring back my wife?)

It is obvious from the above case studies that there are several reasons for elder abuse. It is worth mentioning here that there is a myth that elder abuse occurs only due to economic reasons. This may be true to some extent, but this is not the only reason for this. An analysis of few case studies indicates that "selfish attitude" of the care givers is the main reason of elder abuse.

Marital status, gender status, economic dependency, poor or ill health, weak support systems at the familial and community levels, abusive nature of care givers, rude and demanding nature of care seeker elderly etc. are associated with abuse of the elderly.

It is quite difficult to generalized or come to any conclusion that which factor is more responsible for abuse as it depends on case to case. However, on the basis of case studies and informal discussion and FGD's we may say that elder abuse is taking place in the family mainly due to selfish attitudes of the care givers. With regard to forms of abuse it may be said that verbal abuse and socio-psychological abuse and neglect is very common.

Chapter - 9

Major Findings and Conclusion

This chapter is divided into three parts: Part I presents the major findings of the study, Part II is conclusion and in Part III some suggestions has been offered.

Part I: Major Findings

Elder abuse or abuse of older people by the immediate family members is not a new phenomenon. It remained a private family affair till the last quarter of the 20th century. It is only now that it is recognized as hidden crime whose consequences are varied. Because of abuse the quality of life of elderly people deteriorate.

It is a fact that population ageing is going on, and because of that concern over the abuse or maltreatment of senior citizens has been more heightened in recent times. Several studies have been done on this problem by the scholars all over the world. All these cross-cultural exploratory studies have verified and vindicated the existence of elder abuse. In our country due to several socio-economic change factors, the traditional family/community based support system for the aged has weakened. In some of the states/regions desertion of old parents has come up as a serious problem. The problem is not acute only among the asset less laboring class, it is also acute among the middle classes where the tendency of abuse and neglect of old parents appears to be more due to decline of family values and reckless materialism.

The main focus of the present study was to find out the prevalent types of elder abuse, trends in elder abuse and identify the factors responsible for abuse and the chief abuser. Furthermore, it also aimed at to suggesting measures to prevent elder abuse in the family/ community. The study area was Varanasi. Universe of the study was all the older people of 60+ age who were living at that time in the rural and urban areas of Varanasi. Purposive random sampling method was applied to select 1005 elderly respondents from the universe. For in-depth study, a bunch of case studies has been done to bring out the latent factors/causes of abuse and personal background of the abuser. Before that focus group discussions (FGD's) were organised to know the older persons' views and opinion toward elder abuse and neglect. Through FGDs we were able to identify the abused elderly also. For primary data collection we have used an interview-schedule. Besides this, we have also done several informal interviews with elderly people, knowledgeable persons about them and with respective caregivers just in order to understand the hidden dimensions of the problem.

Socio-economic background of the elderly

Almost a majority (48.2%) of the respondents are of 'young-old' category (60-69 years). Almost half of the total number of them are from urban (50.2%) and rest are from rural background. It was found that the number of young-old is larger in urban areas while of the old-old (80+ years) are concentrated in rural areas. In the sample of the elderly (N= 1005), 83.8 percent were males and only 16.2 percent females. Age and sex-wise distribution of sample clearly shows that majority (53.2%) of the male respondents are in young-old category, while the majority of females (55.2%) are in old-old (70-79 years) category.

The elderly are predominantly Hindu (89.8%). Nearly 45.1 percent of them belong to backward castes and high school is the educational level attained by the largest (25.9%) sub group. Further, while 14.7 percent of them are illiterate, 17.9 percent are just literate i.e. they can only sign their name. More elderly women are illiterate (23.3%) as compared to men (13.1%). Majority (72.3%) of the elderly are married. More men (80.0%) are in the married category while more women (65.0%) are in the widowed category.

Majority (66.7%) of the elderly are living in Varanasi district since birth. More than two-thirds of the elderly (36.0%) are from intermediate and joint family (33.2%) background. The size of the family in the majority (46.8%) of the cases is 7 to 9 members. However, 7.3 percent reported that their family size is as large as 10 and more members. More than 40 percent of the elderly respondents are living with spouse, children and grand children.

A large majority (82.6%) of the elderly live in their own houses. The main occupation of 34.0 percent respondents was service and in 33.0 percent cases the main occupation was related to agricultural work. A majority of respondents (60.0%), who have mentioned their main occupation as service, were working in the informal/unorganized sector. A near majority (45.4%) of the respondents were superannuated 11 to 20 years ago. It is important to note that majority (63.3%) of the respondents are still working, and that too doing unskilled work (30.8%) or cultivation (48.7%). Of the elderly 19.4 percent have no income at all. Around 48.0 percent of the elderly fell in the income range up to Rs. 5000 per month. Only 3.4 percent respondents reported their income more than Rs. 20000/- per month. Sex-wise distribution of the elderly, according to monthly income clearly shows that majority (52.1%) of the female respondents have no independent income at all.

53.9 percent respondents revealed that their close family members are living separately from them. We have received multiple response regarding reasons for separate living of close family members. A large majority (69.0%) of them said it is due to the reason of exigency of service/business and due to sheer selfishness (64.2%).

Majority (98.2%) of the respondents have mentioned health and medical problems as the major problem of senior citizen.

Family life and Socio-Psychological Interactions

The participation of elderly in the decision making process on family affairs is satisfactory. But, it is no less important to note that in the case of 12.4 percent respondents, their advice is not taken on any matter.

A large majority (66.5%) of the elderly don't get the needed nutritious food, not even milk and seasonal fruits. Despite this the majority (73.5%) of the elderly said that their needs were fulfilled by their children.

A large majority (77.3%) of elderly reported that they were getting proper respect from their family members. Only 22.7 percent elderly felt that they were not getting proper respect due to their old (burdensome) age.

A large majority (69.5%) of the elderly don't have the facility of a separate room in their houses and even among 30.5 percent elderly who have a separate room 13.0 percent elderly said that they have to vacate it on a guest's arrival. Though an overwhelming majority (90.0%) of the elderly have their family members' permission to meet guests or receive at home, but the remaining 10.0 percent are denied such facility. In the cases where the elderly persons have no permission to meet guests or have to vacate their rooms to make room for guest, it is quite interesting to know how they feel about it. It is interesting to note that majority (97.5%) of them still like arrival of guests, whatever inconvenience it may mean to them. It is only 2.5 percent elderly who feel dejected.

The caregivers to majority (61.8%) of the male elderly are their wives, while in the case of 42.4 percent female elderly, there is nobody to take care of them.

We have tried to find the sons' or daughter-in-laws' reaction to elderly persons mixing with their grand children. It was found that only in a small percent (5.7%) cases that the sons/daughter-in-laws, dislike the elderly interacting with their children.

With regard to altercation with family members it is found that there are no incidents of conflict in case of 17.9 percent of the respondents, in majority of cases (58.3%) it occurs rarely.

Most of the elderly (94.1%) are satisfied with the facilities provided to them by their families. Most of them (95.6%) are also privileged as their friends visits them off and on. Only 4.4 percent of the elderly say that their friends do not come to meet them. Almost cent percent elderly respondents' relatives do come to visit them. Majority (52.2%) of the elderly respondents also visit their friends houses occasionally. Only 4.4 percent elderly never go to their friends houses. Almost all (95.8%) the respondents' friends get proper hospitality on their visits.

Only 9.3 percent of respondents' relation with their neighbour is cordial, 74.1 per cent's normal, while 9.7 percent respondent's relation is not cordial. In 6.9 percent cases the respondents have no relation with their neighbours.

A very large majority (84.4%) of the elderly are fortunate to have their family members accompanying them to religious/tourist places. However, 15.6 percent elderly are not so fortunate. In their case the reasons vary from lack of personnels or they are too old to travel, but in such visits in 25.5 percent cases it is due to neglect on the part of their family members. A significant proportion of elderly (29.3%) have experienced a decline in the respect given to them within their families. The main reasons are perceived as (a) changing family values (95.0%), (b) selfish attitude of the family members (81.0%) and (c) lack of time with care givers (70.0%), etc. As many as 98.1 percent of the elderly almost unanimously agree that neglect and abuse of elderly is mainly due to disintegration of joint family system.

A very large majority of the elderly (92.2%) do participate in domestic chores. They perform various types of domestic chores like house watch and ward (59.7%), attending visitors/guest (40.0%), watering of plants (38.8%), bringing vegetables, fruits, grocery etc. (38.5%). Only a very few elderly (2.9%) have a servant to take care of them.

Majority (53.9%) of the elderly don't feel neglected. We find that the elderly who are not experiencing neglect by their family members are either the main earners or are in the category of young-old or/and also member of prosperous joint family.

Of all the elderly, 27.1 percent were found unhappy with some or other member of the family. A very large majority (85.5%) of male elderly, and only a little smaller proportion of female elderly (79.2%) are unhappy with their daughters-in-laws. 16 percent of male elderly are unhappy with their wives, while 18.9 percent female elderly are unhappy with their husbands. In majority of cases (66.2%) the main reason of unhappiness is selfish attitude of a particular member (mostly of daughter-in-law and son) and also other members creating tension or problems (62.5%) on several occasions.

As regard to the very idea of staying in Old Age Home during old age, though majority (81.6%) of the respondents were against it, yet a significant (18.4%) percent of them were not averse to staying in Old Age Home.

A vast majority (84.0%) of male and female (71.7%) respondents reported that they never felt isolated. With regard to feeling of loneliness, as experienced by respondents, it was found that 7.4 percent male and 8.6 percent female always had a feeling of loneliness. Majority (68.7%) of the respondents said that old age is the most painful stage of life. A large majority (71.6%) of them have fear of death. Females (49.1%) are less afraid of death in comparison to male elderly (24.3%). Majority (79.0%) of the respondents realizes that there is a change in their behaviour.

Majority (60.1%) of the of the elderly doesn't have pet animals. Majority of the respondents (89.5%) who have pet animals, accepted that due to these pet animals they get some respite from loneliness.

With regard to the main sources of recreation of elderly, a large majority (73.6%) of them watch T.V., News paper is the other important means as 60.7 percent of them like to read it daily. While more elderly women watch T.V., more elderly men read newspapers. The facility of watching T.V. is not available in some rural areas.

Health Status

Majority of the respondents are suffering from the problem of Cataract, Glaucoma and retinal disorders (69.0%), low or high blood pressure (65.2%), dental problem (56.2%), general weakness (52.5%), joint pains, gouts or arthrities (39.5%), diabetes (32.0%).

Cent percent respondents said that it is very difficult to get proper medical treatment. About 60 percent respondent said that it is very expensive and also not easy for an elderly person to consult doctors. However, majority (68.8%) of the elderly gets proper attention and care during illness. 69.2 percent elderly get medicine in time, while 30.8 percent said it is not available to them in time, which is alarming. It is quite alarming that 65.1 percent respondents said that due to their illness their children/ family members pay less attention to taking care of them, they even consider them as burdensome. A large majority

(74.1%) of the respondents don't go for regular medical check up. It is also worth mentioning that not a single elderly female regularly goes for medical checkup. Majority (46.2%) of elderly visit private doctor for such checkups. A very large majority (59.7%) of the elderly said that doctors are not attentive. They don't give proper attention to aged patients. Near majority of the male respondents (47.5%) bear their medical expenses by themselves, while the medical expenses of the majority of the sample female elderly (38.0%) are borne by their husband. An overwhelming majority (90.2%) of the elderly don't have any difficulty in performing their daily routine. Among 9.8 percent respondents who have some difficulty in performing their daily routine nearly one-third (29.1%) of the male elderly get help for doing it by their daughters-in-law. When we compare this with female respondents, 25.0 percent of them don't get help from anyone.

Nearly two-thirds of elderly do chew paan with tobacco (64.5% male and 36.8% female) followed by those, who take Khaini (53.9% male and 51.5% female).

Economic Status and Abuse

19.4 percent elderly have no income at all, followed by around 48 percent having an income of up to Rs. 5000/- per month. Sex-wise distribution by monthly income of the elderly clearly shows that majority (52.1%) of the female respondents have no income of their own, followed by around 36 percent having an income of up to Rs. 5000/- per month.

The main sources of income of elderly are: rental income (32.3%), income from agriculture (30.8%), and service pension (12.7%) etc. 9.7 percent elderly get Old Age Pension/Widow Pension. 16.6 percent elderly earn their income from wage labour. 0.8 percent respondents' family income is nil, which means they are fully dependent on relatives or neighbours. 68 percent respondents' families fall in the monthly income range of Rs. 10,000/- or less. Sex-wise distribution of the elderly by family income clearly shows that majority of female respondents' (54.6%) it is less than Rs. 5000/-. Majority (51.9%) of the families have two earners. With regard to number of dependent members per family, it is reported that the largest segment of them (43.4%) have

4 or more dependents, followed by 32.3 percent having 2 or 3 dependents each.

Almost the total number of elderly have a house (82.6%) or land or housing plot (78.4%) in their names. Sex-wise distribution of the elderly clearly shows that a much larger number of men compared to women reported possession of different kinds of assets. About 45 percent elderly reported that they do have income from the assets.

11.6 percent elderly are in debt. Sex-wise analysis clearly shows that 13.7 percent male and only 1.2 percent of female elderly are having debt. The range of debt amounts shows that the largest number of indebted (51.3%) have incurred debts of Rs. 25000 or less. The maximum amount of debt (Rs. 15 lakh) is on account of home loan. Most of such loans are due on urban elderly persons. While close to a majority (47.5%) of rural elderly has taken loan for the purposes of marriage of their daughters, a large majority (85.7%) of urban elderly have taken loan for house construction.

As regards dependency of elderly who have no personal income (19.4%), we find that majority of them (70.8%) are dependent on their sons. Majority (73.2%) of the elderly are availing facilities provided by the Government to senior citizens. Cent percent of them mainly avail concession on rail tickets. 24.5 percent elderly do avail rebate in income tax.

A majority (63.0%) of the elderly finds that their income is not sufficient to cover their expenses. Most (95.7%) of them manage to meet their shortfall by cutting down expenses or take the help of their sons or daughters.

9.7 percent elderly encountered some sort of threat of dispossession from their property by their family members. Cent percent of the elderly under threat experienced verbal abuse or/and neglect. Almost half of the elderly (47.8%) have already distributed their property among their sons and, in a few cases, their daughters also. Most of the elderly (89.2%) feel neglected after distributing their property. 0.4 percent elderly have been made to sign documents which they could not understand. They can be called victims of financial abuse. Only a few (6.7%) elderly had faced any litigation, but among them 21.4 percent are facing it currently.

Elder Abuse: Forms and Pattern

23.7 percent of the elderly have said that they were being abused. Gender-wise analysis clearly shows that female elderly (43.0%) were more abused than their male counter-parts (20.0%). Among married, a higher percentage (82.4%) was in the 'not-abused' group. Son (45.4%) and daughter-in-law (26.5%) figured as the most frequently mentioned actors in perpetration of abuse against the elderly. If we take male elderly separately, next to son (60.7%), the daughter-in-law (20.2%) figured as the most difficult person to get along with. 5.4 percent have mentioned their wife as chief abuser. On the other side, when we take the female elderly separately, next to daughter-in-law (41.4%), Jethani/ Devrani (17.1%) and husband (14.3%) figured as chief abusers. We have tried to explore reasons for elder abuse. The issues were different for male and female elderly. If we take only male elderly, the discord appeared to centre mostly on issues as demand of money or property (23.8%). More women (57.1%) reported household chores as the main issue of conflict or arguments. Cent percent elderly (100.0%) reported having repeated incidence of verbal abuse. 17.1 percent female and 5.9 percent male elderly reported having experienced physical abuse.

Several forms of abusive behaviour by the abuser have been revealed by the respondents. Physically abuse respondents have to face slapping, pushing/ shaking and physical injury by the abusers. Cheating and stealing of money are the main forms of economic abuse which have to be faced by almost cent percent respondents.

It was revealed that among abused cent percent respondents are facing verbal abuse, socio-psychological abuse and economic abuse almost daily since last 5 years.

Majority (55.6%) of the male respondents have mentioned their reasons for not seeking help during conflict situation as they did not want to disgrace family by seeking help from others, while majority (46.1%) of the females have not informed others in apprehension that they might be subjected to further abuse. Almost equal number (43.1%) of female elderly said that it is of no use as it is part of life, no body will come to help.

An overhelming majority (96.4%) of the elderly are not aware of National Policy on Older Persons. Even the 3.6 percent elderly, who were aware of this policy, didn't know its provisions fully.

Almost all (94.5%) of the elderly said that free medical facilities and governments' economic support (92.0%) is essential to stop elder abuse. Only one elderly has lodged complaint under the Maintenance and Welfare of Parents and Senior Citizens Act, 2007. More than two-thirds (72.7%) of the elderly have not informed anybody about their maltreatment.

Part II: Conclusion

The study is focused on elder 'abuse' in the domestic or family setting. Of course, the family is nestled in the community and larger society settings. Elderly abuse in institutional setting is not part of the study.

For one thing the study clearly brings out that the social malady of elderly abuse in the family setting can not be taken in its face value and its high time that the social policy planners in the country wake up to this stark reality. While weakening of the family system is certainly one major concern in regard to the problem of the aged, it is also becoming evident that the great Indian family system has eroded fast in terms of family values and the incidence of elder abuse in the family may not be as small as it's popularly perceived. But certainly it is not as grave or alarming as made out by various studies. Overall, the incidence of serious cases of elder abuse are rare. So also willful or deliberate cases of gross maltreatment and neglect. Of course, there could be no doubt that there are clear symptoms of the malady becoming manifest in a big way.

The study proceeded on the basis of indicators, mostly qualitative developed so far. Obviously, there is a great deal of subjectivity involved which raises many an analytical problem. Firstly, the meaning given to the indicators by the various respondents is not very uniform. The response is likely to be qualified by the level of living. For instance what a respondent perceives by economic abuse generally, or privacy for that matter would be directly related to the level of living he / she has been used to. For example, the facility of a separate living room for the aged may be alien to the respondents, excepting those belonging to the urban upper middle class. The other equally important subjective factor appears to be the capacity for accommodation, adjustability, sense of self abnegation etc., indeed, the whole attitude on life. Accordingly sense of deprivation, discrimination, denial of basic amenities and expression of resentment on this account would vary from person to person. Yet another aspect of the respondent behaviour is the choice of whom to confide with or complain to. Generally, the respondents don't like to go about discussing their family affairs, much less to complain against their family members, to third persons. The sense of family honour and esteem is still relatively strong in the older generation. To conclude this point, if we were to match families (households) on a set of socio-economic characteristics, the behaviour of the family members towards their elderly is likely grossly vary.

The bunch of pilot case studies, did reveal a greater extent of elder abuse and neglect. Paradoxically the first generation middle class tends to show greater propensity to indulge in elder abuse, and in most cases, willful, as they consider the aged parents, a drag on their rising economic status and standard of life. On the other hand in the poorer classes, there are deprivations but these are shared and even the elderly may not grumble about it.

Though the study has not explored this issue at greater length. But it is clearly indicated that 'systemic abuse', especially of the public health system and social welfare system is endemic. Health is one of the major problem faced by the elderly but the system is hardly responsive and sensitized to the health needs of the elderly. Adequate health coverage is critically important because, the elders actually become burdensome for the family when they get chronically sick, and infirm, and entail heavy medical expenses. Then the chances of abuse also increase. The idea of geriatric medicine is totally missing. There are no separate clinics or service counter in the general hospital for them. Similarly, the social welfare system is more or less oblivious to the needs of the aged persons. Even specially vulnerable category among them eg. the unsupported aged women or widowed or disabled are not covered under any regular universal old age pension.

The study raises a methodological issue. Bringing out the disguided latent phenomenon of elder abuse and neglect needs a more participatory type of relationship between the researcher and respondents. Therefore, it also needs a longer time engagement on the part of the researcher. A respondent would be resistant and refrain from 'opening his heart' to an investigator in a formal interview. As such, the survey method may have some obvious limitations in studying the latent phenomenon of elder abuse.

As the country faces the dilemma of decreasing active-age population, and increasing aged population, the political decision makers and policy planners seem to be most ill prepared to meet the challenge. Most developed countries were able to develop a comprehensive social security system, before they reached this stage, but we are still fiddling with the problem with some piece-meal measures.

Part III: Suggestions

It is observed by Devi Prasad (2008: 195) that, "the elderly victims of abuse require a wide range of supportive, preventive and protective services, backed by changes at policy and programmatic levels. It is a challenged requiring national level planning and co-ordination." For the dignified existence of the elderly the following suggestions has been offered.

(i) Various provision of National Policy for Older Persons (1999) and Maintenance and Welfare of Parents and Senior Citizens Act, (2007) should be operationalized.

(ii) Government Hospitals should have Geriatric OPD and Wards. The Medical treatment of the aged be made cheaper. Their should be provision of mobile medical van for the elderly persons.

(iii) Institutional care to the destitute and physically incapacitated aged be provided by the government. NGOs should be promoted and strengthened in this regard.

(iv) Family counselling is needed to motivate family members to take care of the needs of the aged.

(v) Income tax exemption limit should be raised in the case of those supporting their elderly parents or family members.

(vi) Special flexible working hours should be there for the caregivers especially working female caregivers.

(vii) There is a need to enact a specific legislation (more specific than Maintenance and Welfare of Parents and Senior Citizens Act, 2007) to protect an elderly persons from different forms of abuse and neglect and prosecute offenders through Fast Track Court.

(viii) Advocacy and sensitization towards the needs and problems of elderly should be promoted. Their is a need to enhance community awareness and response towards elder abuse. It is required to educate public not to remain passive spectators. We must promote collective action to stop elder abuse.

(ix) There should be educational and awareness programmes for elderly to reduce the risk of being abused. They should be informed about the programmes and schemes for the welfare of the aged persons. Awareness should be developed among the aged that they can and need to work for themselves. A booklet containing relevant informations about the rights of elderly, legislations, facilities, programmes and provision for elderly people and also what to do and what not to do should be given to each and every elderly persons. Telephone numbers of concerned area police officers should also be made available to all the elderly persons.

(x) For rural elderly, special power should be given to Village Panchayats to stop elder abuse.

(xi) Another important suggestion is that like there should be trained social workers to assist elderly, meals on wheels, free legal aid, free counselling (general and psychiatric) be provided. Planning for graceful ageing by the individual and greater publicity of these plans should be provided by government.

(xii) Their is need to form a special police machinery to protect senior citizens from abuse and crimes against them.

(xiii) Income generating activities should be created for needy elderly and also OAP amount must be enhanced.

(xiv) Community centers for housing elderly should be setup.

(xv) The role of media is very important in this regard therefore, they need to play responsible role to stop elder abuse and neglect.

(xvi) Planning for graceful ageing is also very important for each and every individual, therefore, people should be made aware of this.

Bibliography

Acierno, R. et. al. (2009): Prevalence and Correlates of Emotional, Physical Sexual, and Financial Abuse and Potential Neglect in the United States: The National Elder Mistreatment Study, USA.

Action on Elder Abuse Bulletin, 1995, 11 (May-June). What is Elder Abuse?

Amesur, C.A. (1959). Welfare Services for the Aged and the Infirm, *Indian Journal of Social Work*, 20 (3).

Anetzberger, G. (1987). *The Etiology of Elder Abuse by Adult Offspring.* Springfiled, IL: Charles C. Thomas.

Anetzberger, G.J. Korbin, J.E. & Austin, C. (1994). Alcoholism and Elder Abuse. *Journal of Interpersonal Violence* 9 (2).

Annual Report, (2001). Ministry of Social Justice and Empowerment, Govt. of India.

Antonucci, T. (1990). Personal Characteristics, Social Support and Social Behaviour. In: Binstock R. and George L. (eds.), Handbook of Ageing and the Social Sciences, 3rd ed. USA: Academic Press, pp. 205-216.

Ariela Lowenstein, (2006). Keynote Address in Asia Pacific Roundtable on "Elder Abuse", Organised by International Longivity Centre-India, Govt. of Western Australia and Singapore Action Group on Elders, April 2006, Pune.

Atchley, RC (1977). The Social Forces in Later Life: An Introduction to Social Gerontology, Belmont, CA: Wadsworth.

Avataramu, Ch (2008) Elder Abuse: A Study of Abuse and Neglect of Elderly in Rural Families, Unpublished Doctoral dissertation, Visakhapatnam: Andhra University, Department of Social Work.

Bagchi, Amiya Kumar, 'Globalising India-The Fantasy and The Reality', *Social Scientist*, vol. 22, Nos 7-8, 1994.

Baker AA. Granny-Battering. *Modern Geriatrics*, 1975, 5: 20-24.

Bali, A.P. (1999). Well Being of the Elderly, *Social Change*, 29 (1&2).

Bambawale, U. (1999). Ageing Issues and Challenges: Gender Bias in the Care of the Elderly, *Social Change,* 29 (1&2).

Bandura, A. (1978): Social Learning Theory of Aggression. *Journal of Communication*, 28 (3), 12-29.

Bhat, N. Vignesh (2006). Social Construction of Ageing: An Empirical Study of the Perception of the Urban Elderly, in A.K. Joshi (Ed.) Older Persons in India, Serials Publications, New Delhi.

Bhatia, H.S. (1983). Aging and Society-A Sociological Study of Retired Public Servants, Arya Book Centre, Udaipur.

Biggs, S., Phillipson, C. and Kingston, P. (1995) Elder Abuse in Perspective, Open University Press: Buckingham.

Block, Marilyn R. and Sinnott Jan D. (1979) (eds.) The Battered Elder Syndrome: An Exploratory Study, College Park: University of Maryland, Centre on Aging.

Block, Marilyn R. and Sinnott Jan D. (1979). Elder Abuse: The Hidden Problem, cited in S.K. Steinmetz, Duty Bound: Elder Abuse and Family Care, New Delhi, CA: Sage.

Bonnie, R.J. & R.B. Wallace (2003). Elder Mistreatment: Abuse, Neglect and Exploitation in an Aging America, National Academies Press, Washington DC.

Bonnie, R.J. & R.B. Wallace (eds.) (2002). Elder Abuse: Abuse, Neglect and Exploitation in an Aging America, Panel to Review Risk and Prevalence of Elder Abuse and Neglect, Washington DC: National Academies Press.

Bose, A. and K.D. Gangrade, 'The Ageing in India: Problems and Potentialities, 'Abhinav Publications, New Delhi, 1988.

Bronfenbrenner, U. (1979): The Ecology of Human Development: Experiments by Nature and Design. Harvard University Press.

Bronfenbrenner, U. (1979). The Ecology of Human Development. Cambridge, MA: Harvard University Press.

Bronfenbrenner, U. (1986). Recent Advances in Research on the Ecology of Human Development. In R.K. Silberman, K. Eyferth, & G. Rudinger (eds.) Development as Action in Context: Problem Behaviour and Normal Youth Development. Heidelberg & New York: Springer-Verlag.

Bronfenbrenner, U. (1997). Ecology of the Family as a Context for Human Development: Research Perspective. In J.L. Paul, M. Churton, H. Rossellikostoryz, W.C. Morse, K. Marfo, C. Lavely, & D. Thomas (Eds.), Foundations of Special Education. Pacific Grove, CA: Brooks/Cole Publishing Company.

Burston, G.R. (1975). Granny Battering, *British Medical Journal*, 3:592.

Burstong, G.R. (1977). Do Your Elderly Patients Live in Fear of Being Battered? *Modern Geriatrics*

Carp, F.M. (1999). Elder Abuse in the Family: An Interdisciplinary Model for Research. New York. Springer Press

Census of India, 2001. (2004). *Report and Tables on Age:* Series 1, Delhi: Registrar General and Census Commissioner, 254-60.

Census Of India, 2001. See. www.censusofindia200.org., retrieved on 22/12/ 2010

Chakraborti, Rajagopal Dhar (2004). The Greying of India: Population Ageing in the Context of Asia, Sage Publications, New Delhi.

Chakravarthy, I. (1997). Life in Twilight Years, Calcutta: Kwality Book Co.

Chalk, R. and King, P.A. (1998). Violence in Families: Assessing Prevention and Treatment Programs. Washington, D.C.: National Academy Press

Chanana, H.B. and P.P. Talwar, 'Ageing in India: Its Socio- economic and Health Implications', *Asia- Pacific Population Journal*, 2 (3), 1987.

Channa, H.B. and Talwar, P.P. "Aging in India: Its Socio-Economic and Health Implications". *Asia-Pacific population Journal* 2 (3), September 1987-24.

Chaudhary, D. Paul, (1992). Aging and the Aged: A Source Book, Inter-India Publications, New Delhi, 123.

Chokkanathan, S. & Lee, A. (2005). Elder Mistreatment in Urban India: A Community Based Study, *Journal of Elder Abuse & Neglect*, 17 (2) 45-61.

Chowdhry, D. Paul (1992). Aging and the Aged: A Source Book, Inter-India Publications, New Delhi.

Christopher Foote and Christine Stanners (2002) Integrating Care for Older People-New Care for Old-A Systems Approach, Jessica Kingsley Publishers, London and Philadelphia.

Cliquet, R., and M. Nizamuddin, (eds) (1999). Population Ageing: Challenges for Policies and Programmes in Developed and Developing Countries. New York: United Nations Population Fund and Brussels.

Cohen, Lawrence (2003). Old Age and Global Economy of Knowledge, in Veena Das (Ed.) The Oxford India Companion to Sociology and Social Anthropology, Oxford University Press, New Delhi.

Common Cause, Vol. XXXI, No. 1, Jan-March, 2012, New Delhi.

Cooney, C. and Mortimer, A. (1995) " Elder Abuse and Dementia-A Pilot Study" *International Journal of Social Psychiatry* 41 (4).

Crimmins, E. (1997). Trends in Mortality, Morbidity and Disability: What Should we Expect for the Future of Our Ageing Population. In International Population Conference, Beijing, 1997, Vol. 1. Belgium: International Union for the Scientific Study of Population.

Dandekar, Kumidini (1993) The Aged, Their Problems and Social Intervention in Maharashtra, *EPW*, Vol. XXVII, No. 23, June 5.

Dandekar, Kumidini (1996) The Elderly in India, Sage Publications, New Delhi.

David Held et.al., (1999) Global Transformations, Oxford, Polity Press, 1999.

Davidson, J.L. (1979). Elder abuse. in M.R. Block and J.D. Sinnott, (eds.) *The Battered Elder Syndrome: An Exploratory Study*, College Park, MD: Center on Aging, University of Maryland.

de Jong-Gierveld J., and H. Van Solinge (1995). Ageing and its Consequences for the Socio-Medical System. Population Studies No.29. Strasbourg, France: Council of Europe Press.

Desai, K.G. (1985). 'Situation of the Aged in India" in *Journal of the Indian Anthropological Society*, Vol. 20, No. 3, Nov.

Devi Prasad, B. (1996). Elder Abuse: The Current State of Knowledge, Keynote Address at the National Workshop on Elder Abuse, Chennai: *CEWA*, Chennai, March 16, 1996.

Devi Prasad, B. (2008). Psycho-social Consequences of Elder Abuse and Neglect: A Study of the Implications of Elder Abuse to Mental Well Being Among Rural Elderly of North Coastal Andhra Pradesh, Project Report Supported by ICMR, New Delhi.

Douglas, R. Nickey, T. & Noel, C. (1980). A Study of the Maltreatment of Elderly and Other Vulnerable Adults. Ann Arbor: University of Michigan.

Drury, E. (1994). Age Discrimination Against Older Workers in the European Union. In Studies on the Four Pillars. Geneva Papers on Risk and Insurance: Issues and Practice, No. 73

D'souza, Victor S. (1971). Change in Social Structure and Changing Roles of Older People in India. Sociology and Social Research, 55.

D'Souza, Victor S. (1982). 'The Aged in India' A Paper Presented at the World Assembly on Aging Vienna, 26 July-6 August, 1982.

D'Souza, Victor S. (1989). Changing Social Scene and its Implications for the Aged in K.G. Desai (ed). Aging in India, Ashish Publishing House, New Delhi.

Economic Survey, 2003-2004, p.216, Govt. of India, New Delhi.

Elder, G. & Johnson, M.K. (2002). The Life Course and Ageing: Challenges, Lessons, and New Directions. In R.A. Settersten, Jr. (ed.) Invitation to the Life Course: Towards New Understanding of Later Life. New York.

Elder, G., Johnson, M.K. & Crosnoe, R. (2003). The Emergence and Development of Life Course Theory. In B.J. Lee, J.T. Mortimer & M.J. Shanaham (eds.) Handbook of the Life Course. New York: Plenum Press.

Elsie Chau-Wai and Catherine So-Kum (2004). Elder Abuse by Care Givers: A Study of Prevalence and Risk Factors in Hong Kong Chinese Families in Journal of Family Violence, Vol. 19, No. 5 Oct., Springer Netherlands.

Finkelhor, D. & K. Pillemer (1988). Elder Abuse: Its Relationship to Other Forms of Domestic Violence, in Gerald t. Hotaling, David Finkelhor, John, T. Kirkpatrick and Murray A. Straus (ed.) Family Abuse and its Consequences: New Directions in Research, Sage Publications, Deverly Hills, California.

Finkelhor, D. (1980). Common Features of Family Abuse in James M. Henslin (ed.) Marriage and Family in a Changing Society-Second Edition. The Free Press, New York.

Finkelhor, D. (1983). Common Features of Family Abuse. In D. Finkelhor, R. Gelles, G., Hotaling & M. Straus (eds.) *The Dark Side of Families: Current Family Violence Research*, New Delhi: Sage, 17-28.

Gangrade, K.D. (2000). Studies in Old Age, in M.S. Gore (ed.) Third Survey of Research in Sociology and Social Anthropology, Vol. 1, Published by-ICSSR & Manak Publications Ltd., New Delhi.

Garabarino, J. and Crouter, A. (1978) Defining the Community context for Parent-Child Relations: The Correlation of Child Maltreatment. *Child Development* 49.

Garabarino, J. and Kostelny,K. (1992) Child Maltreatment as a Community Problem. *Child Abuse and Neglect* 16

Gaur and Gaur (2001), "Life Satisfaction Among Institutionalised and Non Institutionalised Elderly" in Ishwar Modi (Ed.) Ageing and Human Development, Rawat Publication, Jaipur.

Gelles, R. & Pedrick-Cornell, C. (1990). Intimate Violence in Families, (2nd Ed.) New Delhi, Sage.

Glendenning, F. (1997) What is Elder Abuse and Neglect: in P. Decalmere and F. Glendenning (eds.) The Mistreatment of Elderly People, New Delhi: Sage Publication.

Goyal, R.S., 'The Problem of Ageing,' *Population Education News*, Vol. 15, No. 6, 1989.

Granahan, D.V., (1972). Contents and Measurements of Socio-economic Development, United Nation's Research Institute for Social Development, New York.

Grundy, E. (1996). Population Ageing in Europe. In Europe's Population in the 1990, David Coleman; ed. New York: Oxford University Press.

Guha Roy S., 'Perspectives on Population Ageing in India,' in S.N.Singh, M.K. Premi, P.S. Bhatia and A. Bose (eds.) Population Transition in India, Vol.1, B.R. Publishing House, Delhi, 1989.

Gujral, I.K., 'Global Ageing and the Role of South Asia,' Key Note Address 'Global Ageing Initiative Summit, Jan. 24, 2001, p.1,obtained through http://www.csis.org/gai/zurich/speeches/gujral.pdf

Gulati, L. and S.I. Rajan, 'Population Aspects of Ageing in Kerala: Their Economic and Social Consequences, 'Paper presented at the United Nations Consultative Meeting on Population Aspects of Ageing, May 1988, New York;

———, 'Social and Economic Implications of Population Ageing in Kerala, India, *'Social Development Issues*, Vol. 13, No. 3, Spring, 1991.

Havinghurtst, R.J. (1960). The Nature and Values of Meaningful Free Time Activity in Tibbitts, C. and W. Donahue (ed.) Aging in Today's Society.

Heller, S. Peter, 'India: Today's Fiscal Policy Imperatives Seen in the Context of Longer-Term Challenges and Risks', IMF/NIPFP Conference on Fiscal Policy in India, 2004.

Hickey T, Dauglass R. (1981). Neglect and abuse of older family members: professional's perspective and case experiences. *Gerontologist* 21.

Hickey, T., and Douglass, R.L. (1981). Mistreatment of the Elderly in the Domestic Setting: An Exploratory Study, *American Journal of Public Health*, 71 (5).

Higuchi, K. (1996). Women in Ageing Society. In Added Years of Life in Asia: Current Situation and Further Challenges, Asian Population Studies Series, No. 141. Bangkok: Economic Commission for Asia and the Pacific.

Himabindu, M. (2002). Human Ageing: Study of Rural Aged Women in Andhra Pradesh, Shipra Publications, Delhi.

Holt, Reinhart and Winston (1985). Domestic Violence, in Crime and Criminology, Sue Titus Reid (ed.) Fourth Edition. The Dryden Press, New York.

Homans, G.C. (1958): Social Behavior as Exchange. *The American Journal of Sociology,* 63 (5), 597-606.

Homans, G.C. (1967) "Fundamental Social Processes in Sociology", ed. by N. Smelser, New York.

Hooyman Nancy R. and H. Asuman Kiyak (1993). *Social Gerontology*, 3rd ed., Allyn and Bacon: Boston.

Hudson MF. Elder Mistreatment: A Taxonomy with Definitions by Delphi. *Journal of Elder Abuse and Neglect*, 1991, 3:1-20.

Hudson, M. (1986) "Elder Mistreatment: Current Research" in K. Pillemer and R.S Wolf (ed.) Elder Abuse in the Family, Dover, MA: Auburn House.

Hudson, M.F. & T.F. Johnson, (1986). 'Elder Neglect and Abuse: A Review of the Literature' In C. Eisdorfer et al. (eds.) *Annual Review of Gerontology and Geriatrics*, 6:81-133, New York: Springer.

Hudson, MF (1991). "Elder Mistreatment: A Taxonomy with Definitions by Delphi." *Journal of Elder Abuse and Neglect* 3 (2); 120.

Humphreys, J., Campbell J, Barrett, S. (1983). Clinical Intervention with the Abused Elderly and Their Families. Thirty Sixth Annual Scientific Meeting of The Gerontological Society, San Francisco, CA, Nov.

Hussain, M.G. (1997) Changing Indian Society and Status of Aged, Manak Publications, New Delhi.

International Labour Office (2000). World Labour Report 2000: Income Security and Social Protection in a Changing World. Geneva.

Irudaya Rajan, S. (2006) Population Ageing and Health in India Centre for Enquiry into Health and Allied Themes, Mumbai.

Jackson, W.A. (1998) Political Economy of Population Ageing, Cheltenham, United Kingdom; and Northampton, Massachusetts: Edward Elgar Publishing.

Jamuna, D. & Padmasree, V. (2000). Psycho-Social Profiles of Abused Elderly, *Indian Journal of Gerontology*.

Jamuna, D. (2005). Issues of Elder care and Elder Abuse in the Indian Context, in Phoebe S. Liebig and S. Irudaya Rajan (Eds.) An Aging India: Perspectives, Prospects and Policies, Rawat Publications, Jaipur.

John Baldock (2001) Caring and Dependency: Age and Disability in Margaret May, Robert Page and Edward Brundson (Eds.) Understanding Social Problems: Issues in Social Policy, Blackwell Publishers, Oxford, U.K.

Joshi, A.K. (2006). Older Persons in India, Serials Publications, New Delhi.

Joshi, AK and Meraj (2009) "Elder Abuse in Domestic Settings" paper presented in 35th All India Sociological Conference, Oct. 10-12, 2009 in University of Kashmir, J&K. (unpublished paper).

Joshi, Arvind K., 'Rural Aged: Living Arrangements, Problems and Care; in A.K.Joshi (eds.) 'Older Persons in India', Serials Publications, New Delhi, 2006.

Kapur, Promila (1997). Elderly Abuse: Some Counseling Tips, *Research and Development Journal*, Vol. 3, No. 3.

Karin Crawford and Janet Walker(2007) Social Work with Older People, Learning Matters Ltd., U.K.

Karlekar, Malvika (2003) Domestic Violence, in the Oxford India Companion to Sociology and Social Anthropology, Edited by Veena Das, Oxford University Press, New Delhi.

Kasthoori, R. (1996) The Problems of the Aged (A Sociological Study). Uppal Publishing House, New Delhi.

Kaur, Malkit. Grover R.P. and Agarwal, Kusum (1987). Socio-Economic Profile of the Rural Aged, in M.L. Sharma and T.M. Dak (ed.) Aging in India: Challenge for the Society. Ajanta Publications, New Delhi.

Kaushik, Archana and Sharma Renu (2005). Integrated Rehabilitation of Elderly and Children, *Social Welfare*, Vol. 52, No. 7.

Kerry Burnight and Laura Mosqueda, 'Theoretical Model Development in Elder Mistreatment', Document No. 234488, date May 2011, U.S. Deptt. of Justice, Funded Grant Final Report. The Regents of the University of California, U.C., Irvine, School of Medicine, Program in Geriatrics.

Khan, AM & S. Handa (2006). Case Studies of Elder Abuse-roots and Bases of Interventions, *Journal of the Indian Academic of Geriatrics*, 2.

Kivela, S. et. al. (1992). *Abuse in Old Age – Epidemiological Data From Finland, Journal of Elder Abuse & Neglect;* 4 (3), 1-18; 1992.

Kohli, A.S. (1996). Research in Social Welfare, New Delhi, Anmol Publications.

Korbin, J.E., Anetzberger, G., Austin, C. (1995). The Intergenerational Cycle of Violence in Child and Elder Abuse, *Journal of Elder Abuse & Neglect,* 7 (1), 1-15.

Korbin, J.E., Anetzberger, G., Austin, C. (1995). The Intergenerational Cycle of Violence in Child and Elder Abuse, *Journal of Elder Abuse and Neglect*, 7 (1).

Kosberg J.I. & J.L. Garcia (1995). Common and Unique Themes on Elder Abuse from a Worldwide Perspective. In: Kosberg JI, Garcia JL, eds. Elder Abuse: International and Cross-cultural Perspectives. Binghamton, NY, Haworth Press, 1995: 183-198.

Kosberg, J.I. & Nahmiash, D. (1996). Characteristics of Victims and Perpetrators and Milieus of Abuse and Neglect. In L.A. Baumhorer & S.C. Bell (eds.) Abuse, Neglect and Exploitation of Older Persons: Strategies for Assessment and Intervention Baltimore, MD: Health Professional Press.

Kosberg, J.I. (ed.) (1983). Abuse and Maltreatment of the Elderly: Cases and Interventions, Bristal, England, John Wright & Sons Ltd.

Kosberg, J.I., Lowenstein, A., Juanita, L.G., Biggs, S. (2003). Study of Elder Abuse in Diverse Cultures. *Journal of Elder Abuse and Neglect*, 15 (3/4).

Kumar, Sanjay (1991). 'Aging of Population: An Investigation in Indian Context' in Indira Jai Prakash (ed.) Quality Aging, Association of Gerontology (India), Varanasi.

Kuppuswamy, B. (2001). Social Change in India, Konark Publishers, New Delhi.

Laches, M.S., Williams, C., O'Brien, S., Hurst, L., & Horwitz, R. (1997). Risk Factors for Reported Elder Abuse and Neglect: A Nine-year Observational Cohort Study. *Gerontologist*, 37 (4), 469-74.

Lachs, M.S., Berkman, L., Fulmer, T., & Horwitz, R.I. (1994). A Prospective Community Based Pilot Study of Risk Factors for the Investigation of Elder Mistreatment, *Journal of the American Geriatrics Society* (JAGS), 42, 169-73.

Lamb, Sarah. (2007). "Modern Families and Independent Living: Reflections on Contemporary Aging" in Sanjukta Dasgupta and Malashri Lal (Eds.) The Indian Family in Transition: Reading Literacy and cultural Texts, Sage Publications, New Delhi.

Lau, E., & Kosberg, J. (1979). Abuse of the Elderly by Informal Care Provides, *Ageing,* 299.

Lee, R.D., W.B. Arthur and G. Rodgers (1988). Economics of Changing Age Distributions in Developed Countries, Oxford: Clarendon Press.

Lowenstein, Doron and Winterstein (2004). quoted in the report of the Asia-Pacific Roundtable on Elder Abuse in April 2006 at Pune by International Longevity Centre- India.

Mahajan, A. (1987). Problems of the Aged in Unorganized Sector, New Delhi: Mittal Publication.

Mahajan, A. (2008). Social Dependency and Abuse of The Elderly, in P. Krishnan and K. Mahadevan (Ed.) The Elderly Population in Developed and Developing World: Policies, Problems and Perspectives, Neeraj Publishing House, Delhi.

Mahajan, Amarjit and Madhurima (1995). Family Violence and Abuse in India. Deep and Deep Publications, New Delhi.

Mallick, Anupriyo (2006). Crime and Older people, *Social Welfare*, Vol. 52, No. 11, Feb.

Mari Bhat, (1992). 'Changing Demography of Elderly in India, *'Current Science*, Vol.63, No.8, Oct. 25.

McLaughlin, J.S., Nickell, J.P., & Gill, L. (1980). An Epidemiological Investigation of Elderly Abuse in Southern Maine and New Hampshire. In *Elder abuse* (Pub. No. 68-463, U.S. House of Representatives, Select Committee on Aging). Washington, D.C.: U.S. Government Printing Office.

Mishra, A.K. and Mishra B.K. (2006). Sociology of Ageing in India: Perspective and Policy Options, in A.K.Joshi (Ed.) Older Persons in India, Serial Publications, New Delhi.

Mishra, Saraswati (1987). Social Adjustment in Old Age, B.R. Publishing Corporation, Delhi.

Mishra, Saraswati (1991). Emergence and Solution of the Old Age Problem, in National Workshop on Pitamaha Sewa (Nov. 1989) Proceedings and Recommendations: Rewa Chinmaya Sewa Trust.

Mohan, R., Inaugural Address at 99th Foundation Day Celebration Function of the Indian Merchant's Chamber, September 8th, 2005, Bombay.

Morgan, Leslie and Kunkel Suzanne (2001). Aging: The Social Context, Pine Forge Press, California.

Mukesh, Ahuja (1996). Widows: Role Adjustment and Violence, Vishwa Prakashan, New Delhi.

Myers, G.C., (1986). Cross-National Patterns and Trends in Marital Status Among the Elderly, Paper Presented to the conference on Aged Populations and the Gray Revolution, Universite Catholique de Louvain, Belgium, Oct.

Nagesh, H.V. (1992). The Problems and the Care of the Aged in India, In Jogam Shankar (ed.) Social Problems and Welfare in India, Ashish Publishing House, New Delhi.

Nahmiash, Daphne (2002). Powerlessness and Abuse and Neglect of Older Adults. *Journal of Elder Abuse and Neglect*, 14 (1)

Nandal, D.S., R.S. Khatri and R. S. Kadian, (1987). Ageing Problems in the Structural Context, in M.L. Sharma and T. M. Dak (eds.) Ageing in India, Ajanta Publications, New Delhi.

Narayanaswamy, S. (2001). Elder Neglect-Some Examples, *Social Welfare*, Oct.

Natesan, Hemalatha (1990). 'Problems of the Aged' in National Symposium of Psycho-Social, Medical and Biological Aspects of Aging (August 9-10 Coimbatore). PSG College of Arts and Science, Department of Psychology.

National Center on Elder Abuse (NCEA). (1998). *The National Elder Abuse Incidence Study; Final Report*, Available at http://www.aoa.gov/abuse/report/default.html.

National Research Council (2001). Preparing for an Ageing world: The Case for Cross-National Research. Washington, D.C.: National Academy Press.

Nayar, P.K.B. (1987). Aging and Society: The Case of the Developed Countries, *J. Social Welfare*, 34 (2).

Nayar, P.K.B. (2004). Elder Abuse and Violence: A Background Paper, Report of First National Seminar on Abuse, Neglect and Violence of the Elderly, Organized by Centre for Gerontological Studies, Kochulloor, Thiruvananthapuram, November 29-30, 2004.

NCEA (2006). Abuse of Adults age 60+: The 2004 Survey of Adult Protective Services, Washington, D.C.

NISD: Age Care in India-National Initiative on Care for Elderly, NISD, Ministry of Social Justice & Empowerment, Govt. of India, Jan 2008, p.1, derived from website http:// nice.nisd.gov.in/pdf/age_care_india_jan08pdf)

Office of the Fayette Commonwealth's Attorney .Elder Crime. Retrieved on 20 December, 2008 from http://www.lexingtonprosecutor.com/elder .HYPERLINK "http://www.lexingtonprosecutor.com/elder%20.htm"htm

Ogg J. & G. Bennett (1992). Elder Abuse in Britain, *British Medical Journal*, 305.

Oh., J., Kim, H. Martins, D. & Kim, H. (2006) A Study of Elder Abuse in Korea, *International Journal of Nursing Studies*, 43 (2).

O'Malley, T.A., Everit, D.E., O'Malley, H.C., and Campion, E.W. (1983). Identifying and Preventing Family-Mediated Abuse and Neglect of Elderly Persons, *Annals of Internal Medicine,* 98.

Padmasree, V. (1991). A Study of Incidence of Elder Abuse and Some Factors Related to Abuse. Master Thesis, S.V. University, Tirupati.

Pajelow, Mildred D. (1989). The Incidence and Prevalence of Criminal Abuse of Other Family Members, in Lloyd Ohlin and Michael Tonry (Ed.) Family Violence, Vol. 11, The University of Chicago Press, Chicago & London.

Parikh, Kirit S. (2002). Social Infrastructure: As Important As Physical Infrastructure, in Parikh, Kirit S. and R. Radhakrishna (ed.) India Development Report 2002, Oxford University Press, New Delhi.

Parra-Cardona, J.R., Meyer, E., Schiamberg, L., & Post, L. (2007). Elder Abuse and Neglect in Latino Families: An Ecological and Culturally Relevant Theoretical Framework for Clinical Practice. Family Process, 46 (4), 451-470.

Patel, M. (2005). The Elderly Victim. *Indian Journal of Gerontology*, 19 (1).

Patel, S. and Krishna Smirit (2007). Abuse and Neglect of Elderly: An Overview, *Social Welfare*, Vol. 54, No.7, October .

Phillipson, C., Keynote Paper on Globalisation and the Future of Ageing: Economic, Social and Policy Implications, Centre for Social Gerontology, Keele University, UK.

Pillemer K., Prescott, D. (1989). Psychological Effects of Elder Abuse: a Research Note. *Journal of Elder Abuse and Neglect*, 1.

Pillemer Karl A., and Wolf, Roaliess (eds.) (1986). Elder Abuse: Conflict in Family, Auburn House Publishing Company, Dover, Massachusetts.

Pillemer, K. & Finkelhor, D. (1988). Prevalence of Elder Abuse: A Random Sample Survey. *Gerontologist,* 28.

Pillemer, K. & Finkelor, D. (1988). Social Isolation and Elder Abuse, *Response,* 1.

Pillemer, K. & Suitor, J. (1992). Psychological Effects of Elder Abuse: A Research Note. *Journal of Elder Abuse and Neglect,* 1 (1).

Pillemer, K. (1986). Risk Factors in Elder Abuse: Results from a Case-control Study. In K. Pillemer and R.S. Wolf, (eds.) Elder Abuse: Conflict in the Family, Dover, DE: Auburn House Publishing Company.

Pillemer, K., & Finkelhor, D. (1989): Causes of Elder Abuse: Caregiver Stress Versus Problem Relatives. *American Journal of Orthopsychiatry*, 59 (2), 179-187.

Pillemer, Karl and J.J. Suitor (1988). Elder Abuse in V.B. Van Hasselt, R.L. Morrison, A.S. Bellack and M. Hersen (ed.) Handbook of Family Violence, New York, Plenum Press.

Pollard, J.H. (1995). Long Term Care in the Selected Countries: Demographic and Insurance Perspectives.

Prabhavathy Devi, N. & Tamilarasi Murugesan P. (2006:2). Institutional Care for the Elderly. *Journal of the Indian Academy of Geriatrics*.

Prabhavathy Devi, N. (2007). Elder Abuse-Ways to Prevent it, *Social Welfare*, Vol. 54, No.7, October.

Prakash, I.J. (1998). Issues in Mental Health and Psychological Well being of Older Persons, in Desai, M. and S. Raju (eds.) Gerontological Social Work in India, Delhi: B.R. Publishing Corporation.

Prakash, I.J. (1999). *Ageing in India,* Geneva: World Health Organisation.

Prakash, I.J. (1999). Living Arrangement of the Elderly in India: Implications for Caregiving, Ageing & Society 1 (3&4).

Prakash, I.J. (2001). Elder Abuse: Global Response and Indian Initiatives, *The Indian Journal of Social Work*, 62 (3).

Purohit, C.K. and Sharma, R. (1972). A Study of Aged 60 year above in Social Profile, *Indian Journal of Gerontology,* 4 (3&4).

Quinn, M.J. and Tomita, S.K. (1997). Elder Abuse and Neglect: Causes, Diagnoses, and Intervention Strategies. 2nd New York :Springer-Verlag.

Rajan Irudaya S., Mishra U.S. and Sharma P.S. (1999). Indian Elderly: Some Views of Populace, *The Indian Journal of Social Work*, Vol. 60, (4) Oct.

Rajan S. Irudaya, U.S. Mishra and P. Sankara Sarma, (1992). 'India's Elderly: Burden or Challenge?', Sage Publications, New Delhi, p.21.

Rajan, Irudaya S. and Kumar Sanjay (2003). Living Arrangements among Indian Elderly- New Evidence from National Family Health Survey, EPW. XXXVIII, No.1, Jan.

Rajan, S. Irudaya, Ageing in Kerala: One More Population Problem?' *Asia-Pacific Population Journal,* Vol. 4, No. 2, 1989;

————, 'Growing Old Gracefully', in K.R.Nair (ed.) *Geriatric Neurology*, Trivandrum Association of Neurology, Trivandrum, 1992.

Raju, S.S. (2002). Health Status of the Elderly: A Medico-Social Study, B.R. Publishing Corporation, Delhi.

Rakesh Mohan, (2004). Fiscal Challenges of Population Ageing: The Asian Experience, Presentation at Global Demographic Change Symposium, 2004, p.302. http:/www kansascityfed.org/publicat/sympos/2004/pdf

Ramamurti, P.V. and D. Jamuna (1999). Elder Abuse in the Indian Context, *Indian Journal of Gerontology*, Jaipur.

Ranjan, R. (1986). Ageing Issues in India, *Sociological Abstracts*, 34.

Rao, K.V. (1995). Rural Elderly in Andhra Pradesh: A Study of their Socio-Demographic Profile. Unpublished Doctoral Dissertation, Visakhapatnam: Department of Social Work, Andhra University.

Rao, Visweswara K., Prasad D.B. and Avataramu Ch. (2000). Attitudes of the Student Youth and Middle Aged Persons towards the Elderly. *The Journal of Social Work,* Vol. 61, Jan. 2000.

Rethi Devi, K. (2006). Elderly Abuse in the Family, in Older Persons in India, Edited by A.K. Joshi, Serials Publications, New Delhi.

Sandhu, Jasmeet and Tripti Arora (2006). Institutionalized Elderly in Punjab-A Sociological Study of An Old Age Home, in A.K. Joshi (Ed.) Older Persons in India, Serials Publications, New Delhi.

Sarkar, B.N., (1989). Demography of Aged People, Indian Academy of Social Sciences, Survey Research Centre, Calcutta.

Schiamberg L.B. & Gans, D. (1999). An Ecological Framework for Contextual Risk Factors in Elder Abuse by Adult Children. *Journal of Elder Abuse and Neglect,* 11 (1).

Schiamberg L.B. & Grans, D. (2000). Elder Abuse by Adult Children: An Ecological Framework for Understanding Contextual Risk Factors and the Intergenerational Character of Quality of Life. *The International Journal of Aging and Human Development*, 50 (4).

Schiamberg, L.B. & Gans, D. (2003). Elder Abuse. In the Encyclopedia of Human Ecology (Vol.1). Santa Barbara, CA: ABC Clio.

Sen Gupta, Amit, 'Globalisation, Reforms and Health Care,' in People's Democracy (Weekly Organ of the Communist Party of India (Marxist), Vol. xxvi, No. 06, Feb. 10, 2002, obtained through internet http://pd.cpim.org/2002/feb.10/02102002_snd.htm.

Sengstock M, Barretts S. Graham R. (1982). Abused Elders: Victims of Villains or of Circumstances? 35th Annual Scientific Meeting of the Gerontological Society, Boston.

Sengstock M, Liang J: (1982). Identifying and Characterizing Elder Abuse. Final report submitted to the NRTA-AARP Andrus Foundation, Institute of Gerontology, Wayne State University, Detroit.

Shah, V.P. (1993). The Elderly in Gujarat, Department of Sociology, Gujarat University, Ahmedabad, (mimeographed).

Shailaja Neelakantan, 'India's Global Ambitions', Far Eastern Economic Review, Nov. 6, 2003, obtained through Internet from Global Policy Forum, p.1. http://www.globalpolicy.org/globliz/special/2003/1106; medicaltourisminIndia.htm.

Shankardass, Mala Kapur (1997). The Plight of Older Women: Victims of Domestic Violence, in Kalyan Baghi (ed.) Elderly Females in India: Their Status and Suffering, Society for Gerontological Research and Help Age India, New Delhi.

Shankardass, Mala Kapur (2010). Elder Abuse and Adult Protection in Ageing and Health in India (eds.) Shanthi Johnson C. and S. I. Rajan, Rawat Publications, Jaipur.

Sharma M.L. and Dak T.M. (eds.) (1987). Aging in India: Challenge for the Society, Ajanta Publications, Delhi.

Sharma S.P. and P. Xenos, (1992). 'Ageing in India, Demographic Background and Analysis Based on Census Materials, 'Occasional Paper No. 2 of 1992, Office of the Registrar General and Census Commissioner of India, New Delhi.

Singh Kanta, Raj Singh and M.L. Sharma, (1987). Problems of Aged Women in Haryana,' in M.L. Sharma and T.M. Dak (eds.). (1987). Aging in India: Challenge for the Society, Ajanta Publications, Delhi.

Singh, Umesh K. (2006). Voluntary Agencies and Care of Aged (A study based on the Institutions for Aged Persons in Varanasi) in A.K. Joshi (Ed.) Older Persons in India, Serial Publications, New Delhi.

Sivaraju, S. (2003). Elder Abuse in a Metropolis: A Study in Mumbai, TISS: Mumbai.

Somayaji, Ganesha (2006). 'Transition, Transformation, and Re-socialisation: A Biographical Approach to the Elderly Question', in Joshi, Arvind K. (ed.), Ibid., 2006.

Soneja, Shubha (2002). "Elder Abuse in India: Country Report for World Health Organisation, HelpAge India, New Delhi.

Soodan Kripal Singh (1975). Aging in India, Minerva Publication, Calcutta.

Srinivas, S. (1996). Elder Abuse: A Study of Abuse and Neglect of the Elderly in Visakhapatnam. Paper Presented at the National Workshop on 'Elder Abuse'. Chennai: CEWA.

Srinivas, S. (2004). Elder abuse: A Study of Abuse and Neglect of the Elderly in Urban Families. Unpublished Doctoral Dissertation, Andhra University, Visakhapatnam.

Srinivas, S., & Vijayalakshmi, B. (2001). Abuse and Neglect of Elderly in Families. *The Indian Journal of Social Work*, 62 (3).

Steinmetz SK. (1988). Duty Bound: Elder Abuse and Family Care. Thousand Oaks, CA, Sage, 1988.

Steinmetz, S.K. (1988). Duty Bound: Elder Abuse and Family Care. Newbury Park, CA: Sage Publications.

Steuer J, Austin E. (1980). Family Abuse of the Elderly. *J. Am. Geriatr. Soc.* 28.

Steur, J. & Austin, E. (1980). Family Abuse of the Elderly, *Journal of the Geriatrics Society*, 28.

Straus M.A, Gelles, R.J. & Steinmetz, S.K. (1980). Behind Closed Doors: Violence in the American Family. New York: Doubleday.

Tayal, S. (1986). The Aged in India, International Conference on Health Policy, New Delhi.

Taylor, P.E. and A. Walker (1996). Intergenerational Relations in the Labour Market: The Attitudes of Employees and Older Workers. In The New Generational Contract, Intergenerational Relations, Old Age and Welfare, A. Walker, ed. London: University College, London Press.

The Ageing and Development Report, HelpAge International, edited by Judith Randel, Tony German and Debrah Ewing of Development Initiatives, Earthscan Publications Ltd., London, 1999.

Thomas, Joseph (2001). Social Movements and Violence, Mittal Publications, New Delhi

Thompson, W.E. & G.F. Streib (1960). Meaningful Activity in a Family Context, in Tibbitts, C and Donahue, W. (ed.) Ageing in Today's Society.

Tina A. Ambani (2006). Inaugural Address, in Asia Pacific Roundtable on "Elder Abuse", organised by International Longivity Centre-India, Govt of Western Australia and Singapore Action Group on Elders, April 2006, Pune. p. 4.

Tondon, Sneh Lata (2001). Senior Citizens: Perspective for the New Millennium, Reliance Publishing House, New Delhi.

U.S. Select Committee (1981). Quoted by Devi Prasad, B. (2008). Psycho-Social Consequences of Elder Abuse and Neglect: A Study of the Implications of Elder Abuse to Mental Well Being Among Rural Elderly of North Coastal Andhra Pradesh, Project Report Supported by ICMR, New Delhi.

United Nations (1999). Ageing in a Gendered World: Women's Issues and Identities. International Research and Training Institute for the Advancement of Women.

Usharani, D. (1989). Old Age Security Values of Children- A Case Study of Scheduled and Non-Scheduled Castes, In R.N. Pati & B.Jena (eds.) Aged in India, Ashish Publishing House. New Delhi.

Veedon, R. (2001). Elder Abuse in the Urban Context. *The Indian Journal of Social Work*, 62 (3).

Venkoba Rao, A. (1996). The Frail Elderlies – Coping with their Needs in Vinod Kumar (ed.) Aging: Indian Perspective and Global Scenario, Proceedings of the International Symposium on Gerontology and Seventh Conference of the AGI, AIIMS, New Delhi.

Vijay Kumar S. (1991). Family Life and Socio-economic Problems of the Aged, Ashish Publishing House, New Delhi.

Vijay Kumar S. and Suryanarayana M. (1989). Problems of the Aged in Rural Sector, (ed.) Aged in India. Ashish Publishing House, New Delhi.

Vijayakumar S. (1999). Elderly in the Changing Traditional Family Structure: An Indian Scenario, *Social Change,* 29 (1&2).

Vijayakumar, S. (1991). Family Life and Socio-Economic Problems of the Aged. Delhi: Ashish Publishing House.

Vinton, L. (1991). Abused Older Women: Battered Women or Abused Elders? *Journal of Women and Aging*, 3 (3).

Vlassoff, M. & Vlassoff, C. (1980). Old Age Security and the Utility of Children in Rural India. *Population Studies,* 34 (3).

Wade, R, Winners and Losers (2001). *The Economist*, April 28th pp. 93-97.

Wadley, Susan Snow (2002). One Straw from a Broom Cannot Sweep, in Diane P. Mines and Sarah Lamb (Eds.) Everyday Life in South Asia, Bloomington Indiana University Press.

Walker, A. (1990). The Economic Burden of Ageing .Orient Long Press. U.K.

Walker, A.J., Martin, S.K. and Jones L.L. (1992). The Benefits and Costs of Care Giving and Care Receiving for Daughters and Mothers. *Journal of Gerontology*, *Social Sciences*, 47.

Ward, R. (1984). Why Survive ? Being Old in America; New York: Harper and Row.

Wiglesworth, A., Mosqueda, L. Mulnard, R., Liao, S., Gibbs, Fitzgerald, W. (2010). Screening for Abuse and Neglect of People with Dementia. *Journal of the American Geriatric Society*, 58: 493-500.

Wolf, R. (1997). *Factors Affecting the Rate of Elder Abuse Reporting to a State Protective Services Program*, Washington, DC: National Committee for the Prevention of Elder Abuse.

Wolf, R., Godkin, M., and Pillemer, K. (1986). Maltreatment of the Elderly: A Comparative Analysis, *Pride Institute Journal of Long Term Home Health Care*, 5 (4).

Wolf, R.S. & Pillemer, K. (1989). Helping Elderly Victims: The Reality of Elder Abuse, New York: Columbia University Press.

Wolf, R.S. (2000). Elder Abuse: An Introduction, *Generations*, 20 (4), 301-5.

Wolf, R.S., & Pillemer, K. (1989): Helping Elderly Victims: The Reality of Elder Abuse. New York: Columbia University Press.

World Health Organization and the International Network for the Prevention of Elder Abuse (WHO/INPEA) (2002) *Missing Voices: Views of Older Persons on Elder Abuse,* Geneva: World Health Organization.

World Population Ageing Report (2007), U.N.

World Report on Violence and Health, edited by Etienne G. Krug et al., WHO, Geneva, 2002, Chapter 5.

Yan, E. & Tang, C. (2004). Elder Abuse by Caregivers: A Study of Prevalence and Risk Factors in Hong Kong Chinese Families, *Journal of Family Violence, 19 (5).*

Appendix

क्रमांक *(गोपनीय/केवल शैक्षणिक कार्य हेतु)*

साक्षात्कार–अनुसूची

वृद्धों के प्रति दुर्व्यवहार एवं उपेक्षाः परिवार में छिपा एक अपराध

प्रो. अरविन्द कुमार जोशी Principal Investigator UGC Major Project No. P-01/546 मो0 9839335199

समाजशास्त्र विभाग सामाजिक विज्ञान संकायकाशी हिन्दू विश्वविद्यालय, वाराणसी–5

0.0 उत्तरदाताओं की वैयक्तिक पृष्ठभूमिः

0.1 नाम (फोन/मोबाइल सहित) :

0.2 उम्रः

0.3 लिंगः पुरुष/स्त्री

0.4 जातिः

0.5 धर्मः

0.6 वाराणसी में कितने वर्षों से रह रहे हैं?

0.7 जिस मकान में आप रहते हैं उसका स्वामित्व किसके पास है?

0.8 आपका मुख्यतः पेशा क्या था? नौकरी/व्यवसाय/प्राइवेट प्रैक्टिस/अन्य

0.9 यदि आप नौकरी करते थे तो नौकरी के सम्बन्ध में विवरण दें–

(i) क्षेत्रः सरकारी क्षेत्र/ निजी क्षेत्र

(ii) सेवानिवृत्ति से पूर्व अंतिम पदः

(iii) कार्य संगठन का नाम व स्थानः

(iv) सेवानिवृत्ति का वर्षः

0.10 क्या वर्तमान में भी आप कोई आर्थिक कार्य/व्यवसाय करते हैं? हाँ/नहीं

यदि हाँ, तो कृपया उसका उल्लेख करे–

0.11 क्या आपकी पत्नी (या आपके पति) कार्यरत थे? हाँ / नहीं

0.12 अपने साथ रहने वाले पारिवारिक सदस्यों का विवरण दें–

क्र.सं.	सम्बन्ध	उम्र	व्यवसाय	आय	वैवाहिक प्रस्थिति	शिक्षा
(i)	स्वयं					
(ii)						
(iii)						
(iv)						
(v)						
(vi)						
(vii)						
(viii)						
(ix)						
(x)						
(xi)						

(यदि और अधिक पारिवारिक सदस्य एक साथ निवास करते हों तो, इसके आगे पुरुषों / महिलाओं / बच्चों की संख्या बता दें।)

0.13 आप अपने पारिवारिक सदस्यों का (लड़कियों सहित) संक्षिप्त विवरण दें। जैसे– कुल बेटे / बेटियाँ

0.14 क्या आपका कोई पारिवारिक सदस्य आपसे अलग रहता है? यदि हाँ, तो कृपया उसका विवरण दें तथा स्प ट करें कि वो क्यों अलग रहता है?

0.15 अलग रहने वाले सदस्य आपसे महीने में कितनी बार मिलने आते हैं?

0.16 क्या आपके (आपकी पत्नी या पति) के नाम अचल सम्पत्ति है? हाँ / नहीं

1.0 पारिवारिक एवं सामाजिक प्रस्थितिः

1.1 आपका अपनी पत्नी / पति के साथ कैसे सम्बन्ध हैं?

सौहार्दपूर्ण / तनावपूर्ण / सामान्य

1.2 क्या आप घर में किसी सदस्य के व्यवहार से दुखी हैं? हाँ / नहीं

(i) यदि हाँ, तो उसके बारे में बतायंकृ–

(ii) क्या आप परिवार के सभी सदस्यों पर विश्वास करते हैं–

यदि नहीं, तो क्यों–

1.3 किन महत्वपूर्ण पारिवारिक मुद्दों पर परिवार के सदस्यों द्वारा आपसे सलाह ली जाती है?–

बच्चों की शिक्षा के सम्बन्ध में/पेशे सम्बन्धी चुनाव के बारे में/वैवाहिक निर्णयों के बारे में/सम्पत्ति सम्बन्धी मामलों में/आर्थिक विषयों के बारे में/परिवार के सदस्यों की व्यक्तिगत समस्याओं के बारे में/अन्य सभी महत्वपूर्ण विषयों में/किसी विशिष्ट मसले पर/कोई सलाह ली ही नहीं जाती।

1.4 क्या आपके बच्चे आपकी आवश्यकताओं की पूर्ति करने का समुचित प्रबन्ध करते हैं? हाँ/नहीं

1.5 क्या आपको परिवार में यथोचित सम्मान प्राप्त होता है? हाँ/नहीं

1.6 क्या आपको ऐसा प्रतीत होता है कि वृद्धावस्था के कारण परिवार के रोजमर्रा के कार्यों में आपकी भागीदारी कम होती जा रही है? हाँ/नहीं

1.7 क्या आप इस घर से अन्यत्र कहीं और भी रहते हैं? हाँ/नहीं

यदि हाँ, तो कृपया विवरण दें..

1.8 क्या घर में आपका अपना अलग कमरा है? हाँ/नहीं

1.9 क्या अतिथियों के आगमन पर आपको उनसे मिलवाया जाता है? हाँ/नहीं

1.10 क्या अतिथियों के आने पर आपको अपना कमरा खाली कर कहीं और रहना पड़ता है? हाँ/नहीं

1.11 क्या किसी अतिथि के आगमन पर आप स्वयं को उपेक्षित महसूस करते हैं? हाँ/नहीं

1.12 परिवार का कौन सा सदस्य आपकी सबसे अधिक देखभाल करता है?

1.13 क्या आपके पुत्र अपने बच्चों के साथ आपका मेलजोल पसन्द करते हैं? हाँ/नहीं

1.14 क्या आपका पारिवारिक सदस्यों के साथ वाद–विवाद होता है? बहुधा/कभी–कभी/अत्यधिक कम

1.15 अधिकांशतया इस विवाद का मुख्य कारण क्या होता है?

1.16 क्या आप अपने परिवार के सदस्यों द्वारा दी जा रही सुविधाओं से संतुष्ट है? हाँ/नहीं

1.17 क्या आपके पुराने मित्र आपसे मिलने आते हैं? हाँ/नहीं

1.18 आप कितनी बार अपने मित्रों के घर जाते हैं?– अक्सर/कभी–कभी/अत्यधिक कम

1.19 क्या आपके मित्रगणों का आपके घर पर वांछित आदर–सत्कार परिवार के सदस्यों द्वारा किया जाता है? हाँ / नहीं

1.20 पड़ोसियों के साथ आपके सम्बन्ध कैसे हैं?– अच्छे / सामान्य / खराब / कोई सम्बन्ध नहीं

1.21 क्या आपके निकट सम्बन्धी व रिश्तेदार आपसे मिलने आते हैं? हाँ / नहीं

1.22 यदि हाँ, तो कब? अक्सर / कभी–कभी / बहुत कम / कभी नहीं

1.23 परिवार के सदस्यों के अतिरिक्त आप अपना खाली समय किसके साथ व्यतीत करना पसन्द करते हैं? पड़ोसी / रिश्तेदार / मित्रगण / एकांत में / क्लब या मंदिर में / अन्य

1.24 क्या आपका परिवार कहीं भ्रमण हेतु जाने अथवा सामाजिक समारोहों व धार्मिक उत्सवों में शामिल होते समय आपको अपने साथ ले जाता है?

हाँ / नहीं

1.25 यदि नहीं तो क्यों?

शारीरिक रूप से अक्षम होने के कारण / घर की सुरक्षा व देखभाल हेतु / आंतरिक मतभेदों के कारण / उचित सामंजस्य न होने के कारण / उपेक्षा व अवहेलना के कारण / अन्य

1.26 क्या आपको लगता है कि परिवार में आपको पूर्ववत् सम्मान प्राप्त है? हाँ / नहीं

1.27 आपके मतानुसार वृद्धों के प्रति परिवार में हो रही उपेक्षा व दुर्व्यवहार के क्या कारण है?

1. परिवार के सदस्य व्यक्तिवादी, स्वार्थी व आत्मकेन्द्रित होते जा रहे है?
2. परिवार पर आर्थिक बोझ बढ़ने के कारण
3. वृद्धों के चिड़चिड़े स्वभाव व अहंवादी तथा रूढ़िवादी होने के कारण
4. परिवार की महिलायें रोजगाररत होने के कारण
5. स्वतन्त्र जीवन में वृद्ध बाधक समझे जाते हैं?
6. अन्य (जैसे वृद्धों की विविध व्यक्तिगत समस्याओं के कारण)

1.28 क्या संयुक्त परिवारों के विघटन तथा माध्यमिक व एकाकी परिवारों के बढ़ते प्रचलन के कारण वृद्धों के प्रति दुर्व्यवहार की समस्या में वृद्धि होगी? हाँ / नहीं

1.29 क्या घरेलू कार्यों में आप अपने परिवार के सदस्यों को वांछित सहयोग देते हैं? हाँ/नहीं

1.30 आप कौन–कौन से घरेलू कार्य करते हैं?

1.31 वे कार्य आप स्वेच्छा से करते हैं या किसी के दबाव में? स्वेच्छा/दबाव

1.32 क्या आपकी देखभाल के लिए कोई नौकर/नौकरानी हैं?
हैं/नहीं है/जरूरत नहीं है

1.33 क्या आप इससे सहमत है कि सामाजिक परिवर्तनों के प्रति सकारात्मक दृष्टिकोण व पारिवारिक मामलों में अहस्तक्षेपनीय मनोवृत्ति वृद्धावस्था में उचित सामंजस्य व सुसंगत जीवन व्यतीत करने में सहायक है?
हाँ/नहीं

1.34 क्या आपको ऐसा लगता है कि परिवार में आपकी उपेक्षा की जा रही है?
हाँ/नहीं

1.35 आपके साथ इनमें से कौन सा व्यवहार होता है? अक्सर गाली दी जाती है/शारीरिक प्रताड़ना की जाती है/मानसिक प्रताड़ना दी जाती है/यौन हिंसा की जाती है/रूपये–पैसों की मांग की जाती है/उपेक्षा की जाती है?

1.36 आपके साथ इस प्रकार का दुर्व्यवहार कब से शुरू हुआ है?

2.0 अवकाश के क्षण:

2.1 क्या आपकी कोई हॉबी है? हाँ/नहीं

यदि हाँ, तो कृपया बतायें–

क–

ख–

ग–

2.2 आप खाली समय किस प्रकार व्यतीत करते हैं?अखबार व पत्र–पत्रिकायें पढ़कर/ व्यापक स्थानों पर जाकर/संगीत सुनकर/मित्रगणों से वार्तालाप करके/टी.वी. देखकर/प्रातः व संध्याकालीन भ्रमण में/फोटोग्राफी, पेंटिंग या बागवानी में/ पूजा–पाठ इत्यादि में/अन्य

2.3 क्या आपको टी.वी. पर अपना पसन्दीदा प्रोग्राम देखने की पूर्ण स्वतन्त्रता रहती है? हाँ/नहीं

2.4 आपके पास इनमें से अपना क्या–क्या है?

टी.वी./मोबाइल/फोन/साईकिल/स्कूटर/कार/अन्य...........

2.5 क्या आपको अपनी हॉबी पूरी करने में किसी प्रकार की कठिनाई का सामना करना पड़ता है? हाँ / नहीं

2.6 यदि हाँ, तो कृपया कारण स्पष्ट करें–

1. शारीरिक असमर्थता के कारण यथा–देखने, पढ़ने या सुनने में कठिनाई
2. कमजोर याददाश्त के कारण
3. आर्थिक पराश्रितता के कारण
4. पारिवारिक सदस्यों के असहयोगी व हस्तक्षेपी मनोवृत्ति के कारण
5. वृद्धावस्था के अनुरूप उचित सामंजस्य न हो पाने के कारण
6. अन्य

2.7 आप अपना खाली समय किसके साथ व्यतीत करना पसन्द करते हैं?

अपने आयु वर्ग के लोगों के साथ / बच्चों या युवाओं के साथ / रिश्तेदारों या पड़ोसियों के साथ / मित्रों के साथ / टी.वी. के साथ / अन्य

2.8 आपके पास कौन सा पालतू जानवर है?

2.9 क्या आप कोई पालतू जानवर पालना चाहते हैं? हाँ / नहीं

2.10 क्या आप ऐसा मानते हैं कि पालतु जानवर अकेलापन दूर करने का अच्छा साधन है। हाँ / नहीं

3.0 शारीरिक व मनोवैज्ञानिक दुर्व्यवहार का ऑकलन–

3.1 क्या आपको निम्नांकित में से कोई शारीरिक अस्वस्थता / बीमारी है?–

मूत्र सम्बन्धी रोग / दृष्टि दोष / सुनने में कठिनाई / पाचन सम्बन्धी शिकायत या भूख न लगना / सामान्य कमजोरी / अनिद्रा / जोड़ों में दर्द या गठिया / श्वास सम्बन्धी तकलीफ / अस्थमा / दमा / रक्तचाप उच्च–निम्न / नकली दाँत / गुर्दे सम्बन्धी तकलीफ / हृदय रोग / मधुमेह / लकवा / कमजोर याददाश्त / कैंसर / अन्य

3.2 यदि आप किसी बीमारी से ग्रस्त हैं तो क्या आपको समयानुसार दवाइयाँ दी जाती हैं? हाँ / नही

3.3 क्या आपकी अस्वस्थता की दशा में घर वालों द्वारा आपकी उचित देखभाल व सेवा सुश्रुषा की जाती है? हाँ / नही

3.4 क्या आप अक्सर तनावग्रस्त / अवसादग्रस्त रहते हैं? हाँ / नही

3.5 क्या आपको ऐसा महसूस होता है कि बीमारी के कारण आपके बच्चे आपको बोझ स्वरूप समझते हैं या बे–मन से आपकी सेवा करते हैं?

हाँ / नही

3.6 क्या आप नियमित रूप से अपने स्वास्थ्य की जाँच कराते हैं?

हाँ / नही

(i) यदि हाँ, तो किससे?

विशेषज्ञ चिकित्सक / सरकारी अस्पताल / निजी अस्पताल / अन्य

(ii) यदि नहीं, तो क्यों? – चिकित्सालय दूर है / आर्थिक पराश्रितता के कारण / परिवार के सदस्यों की उपेक्षा के कारण / कोई लेकर जाने वाला नहीं है / अन्य

3.7 परिवार में आपके साथ किस प्रकार का दुर्व्यवहार होता है?

शारीरिक / मानसिक / आर्थिक / अन्य / कोई दुर्व्यवहार नहीं

3.8 परिवार में अधिकतर दुर्व्यवहार कौन करता है?

पुत्र / पुत्री / बहु / पत्नी / अन्य

3.9 आपका इलाज सम्बन्धी खर्च कौन वहन करता है? स्वयं / बेटा / अन्य

3.10 क्या आपको दैनिक कार्यों की पूर्ति में किसी प्रकार की कठिनाई होती है?

हाँ / नही

यदि हाँ, तो इसमें आपकी सहायता कौन करता है?

बेटा / बहू / नौकर / दाई / ....

3.11 क्या आपको अपनी उम्र के अनुसार पौष्टिक व संतुलित आहार प्राप्त होता है? हाँ / नही

3.12 क्या आप दूध व मौसमी फलों का सेवन करते हैं? हाँ / नही

3.13 क्या आप अपने बच्चों के साथ रहते हुए अलग खाना बनाते हैं?

हाँ / नही

3.14 क्या आपको अकेलापन महसूस होता है? हाँ / नही

3.15 क्या आपको घर से बाहर समय व्यतीत करना ज्यादा अच्छा लगता है?

हाँ / नही

3.16 क्या अपनी दिनचर्या में बाधा आने पर आप खीज जाते हैं? हाँ / नही

3.17 क्या आपको लगता है कि यह आपके जीवन की सर्वाधिक कष्टदायी अवस्था है? हाँ / नही

3.18 क्या आपको मृत्यु का भय सताता है? हाँ/नही/कभी–कभी

3.19 क्या आपको ऐसा लगता है कि उम्र बढ़ने के साथ–साथ आपके व्यवहार में बदलाव आया है? हाँ/नहीं

4.0 आर्थिक स्थितिः

4.1 आपकी आय के स्त्रोत क्या हैं?

पेंशन/फिक्स डिपोजिट/किराये से आय/अन्य (जैसे– वृद्धावस्था पेन्शन)

4.2 सेवानिवृत्ति के समय आपको क्या–क्या सुविधायें प्राप्त हुई थीं?

CPF/GPF/ ग्रेच्युटी/पेंशन/चिकित्सा सुविधा

4.3 यदि वर्तमान में आप पेंशन प्राप्त कर रहे हैं तो कृपया विवरण दें–

(i) लगभग कितनी पेंशन आप पाते हैं–

(ii) जीवन साथी की कोई आय हो तो बतायें–

(iii) क्या आपको पेंशन लेते समय किसी प्रकार की कठिनाई का सामना करना पड़ता है? हाँ/नही

4.4 क्या आप सरकार द्वारा वरिष्ठ नागरिकों को दी जाने वाली सुविधाओं का लाभ आप प्राप्त कर रहे हैं? हाँ/नहीं

यदि हाँ, तो कृपया विवरण दें कि निम्नांकित में से क्या–क्या लाभ लेते हैं?

आय कर में छूट/यात्रा शुल्क में कटौती/उच्च ब्याज दर /मुफ्त चिकित्सा/अन्य......

4.5 आप पर कितने पारिवारिक सदस्य आर्थिक रूप से आश्रित हैं?

4.6 क्या आपकी आय खर्चों की दृष्टि से– पर्याप्त/बराबर/कम है।

4.7 यदि आय खर्चों से कम है तो ऐसी स्थिति में आप किस प्रकार सामंजस्य करते हैं?

खर्च में कटौती करके/पुत्र–पुत्रियों या रिश्तेदारों द्वारा प्राप्त आर्थिक सहायता से/कर्ज लेकर/अन्य

4.8 क्या आपके परिवार के सदस्य अथवा निकट सम्बन्धी आपकी सम्पत्ति हड़पने के लिए आप पर अनावश्यक दबाव डालते हैं? हाँ/नही

4.9 उनका दबाव किस रूप में प्रकट होता है? वाक दुर्व्यवहार/धमकी/शारीरिक प्रताड़ना/छोटी–छोटी आवश्यकताओं की पूर्ति रोककर/भावनात्मक दबाव बनाकर/अन्य

4.10 क्या आपने अपनी सम्पत्ति में पुत्रों/पुत्रियों को हिस्सा दे दिया है? हाँ/नही

4.11 यदि हाँ, तो क्या हिस्सा देने के पश्चात् आप पूर्व की अपेक्षा स्वयं को उपेक्षित महसूस करते हैं? हाँ/नही

4.12 कभी आपके व पारिवारिक सदस्यों के बीच सम्पत्ति सम्बन्धी विवाद या मुकदमेबाजी हुई हैं? हाँ/नही

4.13 क्या वर्तमान में आपका कोई मुकदमा चल रहा है? हाँ/नही

4.14 क्या वृद्धावस्था में व्यक्ति को घर परिवार से दूर 'ओल्ड एज होम' में रहना चाहिए? हाँ/नही

4.15 क्या आप 'ओल्ड एज होम' में रहना पसंद करेंगे? हाँ/नही

4.16 क्या आप वृद्धों सम्बन्धी राष्ट्रीय नीति से परिचित हैं? हाँ/नही

4.17 आपके अनुसार वृद्धों की सबसे बड़ी समस्या और उसका समाधान क्या है?

4.16 यदि आप ऐसे किसी वृद्ध को जानते हों जिसके साथ पारिवारिक दुर्व्यवहार होता हो तो, कृपया उसका संक्षिप्त विवरण दें–

4.17 आपके अनुसार वृद्धों के प्रति बढ़ रही पारिवारिक दुर्व्यवहार एवं उपेक्षा की घटनाओं को रोकने के लिए सरकार को क्या प्रावधान करने चाहिए?

4.18 क्या आपने वृद्धों के प्रति दुर्व्यवहार को रोकने के लिए या समुचित देखरेख एवं संरक्षण के लिए 2007 के कानून का सहारा लिया है? हाँ/नहीं

4.19 क्या आप, अपने साथ हो रहे दुर्व्यवहार की सूचना किसी को देते हैं?
कोई दुर्व्यवहार नहीं हो रहा है/पुलिस को/पड़ोसी को/रिश्तेदार को/घर के किसी सदस्य को/किसी को भी नहीं

4.20 क्या आपने किसी ऐसे दस्तावेज पर हस्ताक्षर किये हैं जो कि आप की समझ से परे रहा हो? हाँ/नहीं

4.21 वृद्धों के साथ हो रहे दुर्व्यवहार या उपेक्षा के सन्दर्भ में यदि और कुछ आप कहना चाहते हैं तो कृपया उल्लेख करें–

Index

T

U

V